I0813398
TO:
FROM:
DATE:

God
Is So
Good

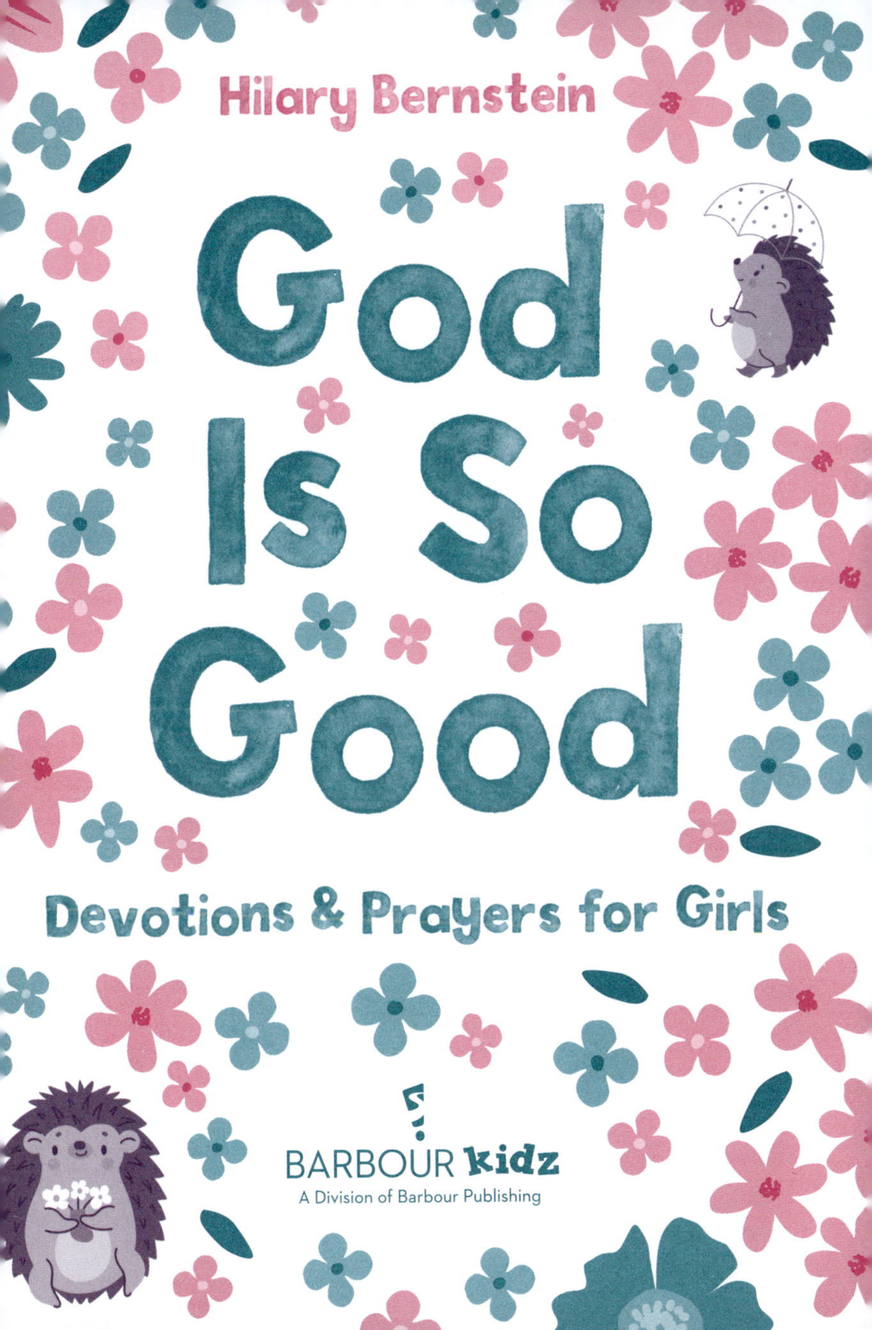

Hilary Bernstein

God Is So Good

Devotions & Prayers for Girls

BARBOUR kidz
A Division of Barbour Publishing

Print ISBN 979-8-89151-153-8

Published by Barbour Publishing, Inc., 1810 Barbour Drive, Uhrichsville, Ohio 44683, www.barbourbooks.com

Our mission is to inspire the world with the life-changing message of the Bible.

ecpa Member of the Evangelical Christian Publishers Association

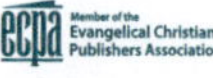

Printed in China.

002552 0725 HA

Introduction

Whether you realize it or not, you were created with purpose in an amazing way. God knew every detail about you long before you were born, and in His goodness, He planned for you to live right here and right now.

He wants to do special things through you and your life—things He has already planned for you to do. You belong right now in all of time and history. You belong right where you are. And you belong in God's family. He has so many wonderful plans for you!

Feel free to be the girl God created you to be, even when it means you won't fit in with the world. Instead of worrying about what others think of you, know that your heavenly Father loves you so very much and He'll never leave you on your own. He has given you much more than you can even imagine and wants to keep filling your life with good things!

Chosen!

God has chosen you. You are holy and loved by Him. Because of this, your new life should be full of loving-pity. You should be kind to others and have no pride. Be gentle and be willing to wait for others.

Colossians 3:12

Everyone knows the thrill of being chosen, whether you have made the team or been selected for a special list or been picked as a friend.

The amazing news is that through Jesus, God has chosen you. You're on His team. You've made His list. Jesus is your friend. You didn't earn this favor through your talents and abilities. It doesn't matter what you look like or who your family is. He chose you. *You!*

The fact that the God of the universe chose you is amazingly special. He loves you dearly. Because He chose you and set you apart to be His own, you should act and feel differently. You're chosen by the Lord God Almighty.

Lord, thank You for choosing me! Please help me live differently because of Your amazing gifts.

Loved

But I have trusted in Your loving-kindness.
My heart will be full of joy because You
will save me. I will sing to the Lord,
because He has been good to me.

PSALM 13:5–6

You know that feeling when something really good happens to you, and you just can't wait to tell someone else? When you think about what God has done for you, you can experience that same amazingly happy feeling.

He loves you so very much just for being you, and His love doesn't stop, it doesn't change, it doesn't depend on you and your moods or on His moods.

Think about something or someone you love the most. Then take that love and multiply it by a million. God loves you even more than that. To know you mean that much to God is pretty amazing. And it's something to get excited about!

Heavenly Father, I praise You for the amazing way You work in my life! Thank You for Your love.

Childlike Faith

Jesus called the followers to Him and said, "Let the little children come to Me. Do not try to stop them. The holy nation of God is made up of ones like these."

LUKE 18:16

For most of your life, you might have heard someone tell you to grow up. Or you've told yourself you need to act older. While growing up is a natural part of life, it's not always a good thing. In fact, Jesus taught that believers should have childlike faith.

What does that mean? While having a childlike faith doesn't mean having a childish faith, it does mean you don't need to have everything figured out. What you do need to do, though, is run to Jesus at any time for any reason. He's so glad when you come to Him in faith!

Father, I'm glad You know my heart and my faith in You. I don't have to know a bunch of deep answers. I just have to know and trust Jesus.

See Your Blessings

The Lord is all that I am to receive, and my cup. My future is in Your hands. The land given to me is good. Yes, my share is beautiful to me. I will give honor and thanks to the Lord, Who has told me what to do. Yes, even at night my mind teaches me.

PSALM 16:5–7

Our Lord loves to give good gifts to those He loves. And once you're part of His family through Jesus, He definitely loves you. He makes things work in your favor. He continually watches over you and protects you. He guides and directs you during the day when you're listening to Him and even in the night when you don't realize it.

When you notice all the big and small ways God is showing His care and concern with His blessings and good gifts, thank Him!

Father, thank You for loving me so much that You give me really good gifts and plan wonderful things for me. You are so very good to me!

The Power of God

Christ's weak human body died on a cross. It is by God's power that Christ lives today. We are weak. We are as He was. But we will be alive with Christ through the power God has for us.

2 CORINTHIANS 13:4

If you make a list of all your strengths and weaknesses, chances are it's easy to pinpoint all of your failures and flaws. Even if you wish you were perfect, imperfection is a part of life. Absolutely everyone has weaknesses.

When you trust Christ as your Lord and Savior, you receive a lot of great gifts, like forgiveness and forever life. You'll also be filled with God's power. You still might feel weak, but with Him working through you, you'll be strong. His power and strength will be a part of you as you learn to rely on Him.

Lord, Your power is amazing.
Thank You for sharing it with me!
I may be weak, but You'll make me strong.

Waiting in Hope

Our soul waits for the Lord. He is our help and our safe cover. For our heart is full of joy in Him, because we trust in His holy name. O Lord, let Your loving-kindness be upon us as we put our hope in You.

PSALM 33:20–22

Waiting can seem so very hard! Whether you're waiting on something that you're really looking forward to or waiting for something uncomfortable to be over, patience is difficult!

When things in this world make you feel out of sorts—you might feel scared or worried or angry about things that are happening now or might happen in the future—patience seems almost impossible. Yet when you step back and remember who God is, it's possible to wait in hope. He is your help! He is your safe cover. His name and His character are worthy of your trust. Because His love never fails, you can rejoice in Him and wait for Him.

Father, I may not like waiting, but I'm really glad I can wait in hope for You. Please help me patiently wait for You to work out Your very good plans.

Out of the Dark

But you are a chosen group of people. You are the King's religious leaders. You are a holy nation. You belong to God. He has done this for you so you can tell others how God has called you out of darkness into His great light.

1 PETER 2:9

When you consider all that God has done for you and how highly He thinks of you, it's pretty amazing. He has called you out of darkness into His wonderful light. He has chosen you to be His own. In His eyes, you're royal (you're now the daughter of the King of kings!) and holy. On top of all of that, you belong to Him.

That kind of goodness should give you a reason to praise God! He knows exactly who you are and what you do and still thinks you're amazingly special. Have you thanked Him for the kind ways He shows you favor? Have you praised Him for His goodness and kindness and love?

Father, You are so very good to me! Thank You for choosing me and adopting me into Your family.

Part of His Plan

We were already chosen to be God's own children by Christ. This was done just like the plan He had. We who were the first to put our trust in Christ should thank Him for His greatness.

EPHESIANS 1:11–12

Some people like to think of the big picture, while others are detail oriented. The world definitely needs both big-picture and detail-oriented people.

It should come as no surprise that God is God, and as Creator of all, He knows both the big picture and every single detail. He has a plan for every person and everything that happens in the universe. And you are part of His plan.

The great thing is that God keeps working out absolutely everything to go along with His purpose and plan. Every single detail works as a part of His plan. He's never surprised. He never wonders what will happen next. He knows the end from the beginning because He has the power and might to plan it all.

Lord God, I may not know what's happening in my future, but You do! I'm really thankful I can trust You.

Happily Ever After

Then I saw a new heaven and a new earth. The first heaven and the first earth had passed away. . . . I heard a loud voice coming from heaven. It said, "See! God's home is with men. He will live with them. They will be His people. God Himself will be with them. He will be their God."

REVELATION 21:1, 3

You might feel like you belong here on earth, but this world won't last forever. The Bible tells us that everything will be replaced with new heavens and a new earth. In this new home, you won't be separated from God. His dwelling place will be with you!

That's spending eternity with the King of kings and Lord of lords. That's a forever relationship with the Maker of heaven and earth. That's spending the rest of time in a new place with the Creator of all. That's living happily ever after!

Father, I don't know exactly what it will be like to spend forever with You. But I'll get to see You, worship You, and be with You. Thanks for including me as part of Your perfect plan!

Seen and Heard

The eyes of the Lord are on those who do what is right and good. His ears are open to their cry.

PSALM 34:15

Sometimes, you might feel like no one notices you. People look past you, or they don't listen to a word you say. But God sees you. In fact, He sees every bit of what's going on in your life. He hears you too, including every word you say and even every thought you think. Not a single bit escapes His notice. Because He made you, He understands what you're going through and how you're handling things.

Since your heavenly Father is right here paying attention to you with great love and care, you don't need to be afraid to talk to Him. Open up with all of your thoughts and feelings. Pour out your heart to Him, knowing He does listen. His eyes are on you, and you can find comfort and help through Him.

Lord, thank You for seeing me! Thank You for hearing me! Thank You for knowing me completely and choosing to love me anyway.

The Best Helper

"Then I will ask My Father and He will give you another Helper. He will be with you forever. He is the Spirit of Truth. The world cannot receive Him. It does not see Him or know Him. You know Him because He lives with you and will be in you."

JOHN 14:16–17

After Jesus was crucified, dead, buried, resurrected, then returned to heaven, it didn't seem like He would be with His followers anymore. But He knew He wasn't leaving them alone.

He left His Helper, the Holy Spirit. This "Spirit of Truth" becomes a part of you when you believe in Christ. It's like He moves in as an assurance that you're now the Lord's. Once He is living inside you, He'll be with you forever, leading, guiding, and helping you as you listen to Him and honor Him.

Lord, thank You so much for the gift of Your Holy Spirit! I'm glad He'll never leave me. I'm glad He'll be with me forever! Please help me to know Him and honor Him more and more.

Beautiful!

He has made everything beautiful in its time. He has put thoughts of the forever in man's mind, yet man cannot understand the work God has done from the beginning to the end.

ECCLESIASTES 3:11

Could something that is ugly be considered beautiful? While it might surprise you, of course it could! Beauty often can be hidden. Yet God works behind the scenes, transforming even the ugliest parts of this world into something beautiful that will bring Him honor and glory.

Sometimes you might see the transformation with your own eyes, and you'll be surprised by the miracles God has performed. But at other times, you'll just have to trust that He's in the middle of bringing beauty into the most hideous spaces. As the master artist, He has a method behind His masterpiece. And when He's finished, it will be astonishingly beautiful!

Lord, I'm amazed that You will make absolutely everything beautiful in its own time. I'm excited to watch Your work and see Your progress!

Ordinary People

"I have let you live so you could see My power and so My name may be honored through all the earth."

EXODUS 9:16

When you consider yourself and how you're just a normal girl, you may be pretty astonished to realize that God can show you His power in amazing ways. He can even use you to be a part of His plan!

God used a normal man like Moses to confront Pharaoh and bring amazing wonders to the Egyptians. Moses didn't have any power on his own, but the Lord worked through him.

You don't have any power on your own either. But God can work through you. And if you're willing to be used by Him, He can work through you in amazing ways!

How can you begin this process? Simply ask Him! Thank Him for His power, then ask Him to use you in a mighty way for His glory. Get ready to watch the way He'll work!

Father, thank You for showing Your power through ordinary people. Please use me and my life to glorify You!

Really Good Gifts

Whatever is good and perfect comes to us from God. . . . He gave us our new lives through the truth of His Word only because He wanted to.

JAMES 1:17–18

Really thoughtful gifts are such a treat to receive! Not much can compare to feeling like the gift giver thought about exactly what you want or need and then surprised you with a perfect gift.

Just as good gifts are special to open and appreciate, so are God's gifts. He is filled with love and generosity, and He pours out that thoughtful care to you with His perfect gifts. He might surprise you with something you've always hoped for or dreamed about, or He might give you something really wonderful that you never even imagined.

You're His prized possession, and because of that, He delights in you. He shows some of that delight in the way He fills your life with wonderful things you could never buy or even earn on your own.

Father, thank You for Your good gifts! You know me so well. I'm thankful for the ways You surprise me!

Enemies to Friends

At one time you were strangers to God and your minds were at war with Him. Your thoughts and actions were wrong. But Christ has brought you back to God by His death on the cross. In this way, Christ can bring you to God, holy and pure and without blame.

COLOSSIANS 1:21–22

When people oppose you, it's easy to consider them as enemies. Especially if a person has gone out of her way to alienate herself from you, it's tempting to hold a grudge and guard yourself from getting hurt.

Before you knew Jesus, you were alienated from God. Your sins proved you were His enemy. But Jesus changed all of that. Once you stepped out in faith and accepted Him as Lord, He made you right with God. Now you're seen as holy instead of evil. You belong instead of being an outsider. You're God's friend and daughter. You aren't His enemy anymore.

Jesus, thank You for changing my relationship with the Father! Through You, I'm accepted.

My Forever Home

But we are citizens of heaven. Christ, the One Who saves from the punishment of sin, will be coming down from heaven again. We are waiting for Him to return. He will change these bodies of ours of the earth and make them new. He will make them like His body of shining-greatness.

PHILIPPIANS 3:20–21

It can be tough to remember that this world isn't your forever home. But it's not.

As long as you choose to trust in Christ, you have a future with Him in heaven. You will belong there with Him, where you'll actually get to see Him. Once you're there, He'll change you. You'll have a glorious new body that won't be weak or frail. Your body won't get hurt, and you won't have to think about getting old or dying. Nothing will seem out of place or chaotic or stressful anymore. Instead, everything will be brought under His control. That's a place worth staying in forever!

Jesus, I'm glad You'll return someday. I'm glad You'll change my body into something glorious and eternal. And I'm glad I'll get to worship You face-to-face!

No More Fear!

"Do not fear, for I am with you. Do not be afraid, for I am your God. I will give you strength, and for sure I will help you."

Isaiah 41:10

What are you afraid of? When you think of fears and phobias, what scares you?

No matter what sends shivers up your spine, know that the Lord can free you from fear. That's right! Through Him, you don't have to fear. You don't have to be dismayed. You don't have to worry.

So how can you be free from fear through the Lord? When you have a relationship with Him, He's with you. His Holy Spirit fills you and helps you. He strengthens you in an amazing way. And your fear? It vanishes in His presence. His strength and peace flood you like nothing else, and you can live a life of courage and strength.

Father, thank You for Your strength! Thank You for Your courage! It is such a huge relief to know that, through You, I don't have to fear anymore!

Seen

So Hagar gave this name to the Lord Who spoke to her, "You are a God Who sees."

GENESIS 16:13

It can be easy to feel invisible, like everyone forgets about you and your opinion. You can feel overlooked and passed up, even when you try to speak up.

But God? He notices you. In fact, He's the God who sees you! He sees what you're going through. He hears your prayers. He knows when you're having a good day and when your day is one of the worst you've had. He's always there, always seeing, always knowing.

The next time you feel alone and forgotten, tell the Lord about it. Honestly pour out all your feelings to Him. Not only will you be seen, but you'll also be heard.

Father God, I am so glad You are the God who sees me. Thanks for never leaving me alone. Thank You for caring about me and what I'm facing.

Just like Jesus

Do as God would do. Much-loved children want to do as their fathers do. Live with love as Christ loved you. He gave Himself for us.

Ephesians 5:1–2

If you try to imitate someone, you need to pay attention and notice tiny details. To repeat what someone says word for word, listen closely. And to become more like someone else, focus on what they do and how they act.

As a deeply loved child of God, a way to show your love and gratitude is to imitate Jesus. He lived a perfect life, and even though you'll never be perfect like Him on this earth, it's still a great goal to follow His ways. He's the one to copy. He's worth imitating. Just as His life was filled with love for others, the best way to follow Him is to be filled with love for others too.

Jesus, I want to be like You. Please help me love others like You love. Please help me give of myself for others just like You did.

Filled with His Love

"I have loved you just as My Father has loved Me.
Stay in My love. If you obey My teaching,
you will live in My love. In this way, I have obeyed
My Father's teaching and live in His love."

JOHN 15:9–10

Everyone wants to be loved, but love can seem tricky. People you want to love may not share your same feelings. And other people? Even when they love you unconditionally, it doesn't feel like their love fulfills.

But the love God has for you? It fills any emptiness you feel. The love Jesus poured out for you is immense. It's the one thing that actually satisfies your need for love.

Once you're filled with His love, you can start sharing it with others. You can remain in His love; it doesn't fade away. It won't disappear and leave you alone. That kind of love from Jesus can't be faked or forced. It's the real deal. And it's amazing.

Jesus, thank You for loving me like the Father has loved You. I want to stay in Your love forever!

Trust Him

Trust your work to the Lord, and your plans will work out well.

PROVERBS 16:3

It can be fun to dream about your future, like who you might marry or what kind of job you'll have or what amazing places you'll see. Sometimes you can even use those hopes to help you set goals for your life. But as much as you plan your future, keep a few things in mind.

First of all, plans aren't certain. Just because you'd like to prepare for something doesn't mean it will become a reality. Second, you can dream all you'd like, but the Lord is the one who will establish your plans.

As you remember that God is the one in control and commit to Him all the things you're doing and would like to do, He'll guide your dreams and plans. He might even make them a reality!

Lord, You know my heart. You know my deepest hopes and my greatest dreams. I pray that I'll listen to Your leading. I want to honor You with what I do.

Freedom!

Now, because of this, those who belong to Christ will not suffer the punishment of sin. The power of the Holy Spirit has made me free from the power of sin and death. This power is mine because I belong to Christ Jesus.

ROMANS 8:1–2

Look around and you'll spot condemnation everywhere. Are you different from other people? You might face judgment. Do you disagree with someone else's opinion? You might get ridiculed. Have you stood up for your beliefs? You might feel like an outsider.

But when you belong to Jesus, He won't condemn you. Instead, you'll experience His acceptance. You don't have to feel like a prisoner tied to the unforgiving consequences of your sins. Because of Jesus, you're truly free. No more judgment. No more ridicule. No more life on the outside. Because of Jesus, you don't have to worry about facing punishment and death.

Lord Jesus, Your freedom is an amazing gift! Thank You for rescuing me from the cycle of sin, condemnation, and death. Thank You for Your true freedom!

Very Good Plans

O Lord, You are my God. I will praise You. I will give thanks to Your name. For You have been faithful to do great things, plans that You made long ago.

Isaiah 25:1

Planning ahead can be really helpful. But even your best plans aren't guaranteed. Life can change in the blink of an eye and your thoughtful plans can seem ruined.

God's plans are different. He made plans for your life long, long ago, and He's working them out even right now. He's faithfully in the middle of doing wonderful things for you and with you. Even if things don't seem to be perfect right now, you can trust Him and His very good plans. And you can praise Him for the wonderful things He's doing in your life!

Father, it's pretty amazing to consider that You've made plans for me. I can hardly wait to see what they are!

Tears in a Bottle

You have seen how many places I have gone.
Put my tears in Your bottle. Are they not in Your book?
Psalm 56:8

When you're having a bad day, it's easy to feel like you're all alone. But you're not alone. In fact, God pays attention to every tiny detail of you and your life. He keeps track of all of your sorrows. (He pays attention to what brings you joy too!) He collects all your tears. He knows what breaks your heart, and He knows exactly why you're crying.

In all of your disappointment and sadness, the Lord sees you. He hears you. He knows your heart. And if He could wrap His arms around you to hold you tight as you cry, He would. He loves you. He wants the best for you. And He is there for you.

Father, it's hard to grasp that You actually keep track of what makes me sad. Thank You for not just noticing me but for caring so very much for me.

Waiting for Something Better

But they wanted a better country. And so God is not ashamed to be called their God. He has made a city for them.

HEBREWS 11:16

Ever feel like you don't completely fit in with this world? Or even like you don't fit in with your friends or family?

The thing is, you're only here on this earth for a little while. You're passing through on your way to your permanent home where you really do belong. God has prepared this better, forever home for you, and you'll fit into your heavenly home perfectly.

You can make the most of your time here by remembering you're on a journey. Then, every time you feel out of place, remember this world isn't your home. God has prepared your heavenly home, and you're just waiting to move in!

Father, when I feel out of place here, please help me remember it's because I'm waiting for my forever home. I don't have to fit in right now!

Always Have Hope

As for me, I will always have hope and I
will praise You more and more.

Psalm 71:14

Have you ever considered what it would be like to always have hope? That's confidently trusting always and forever.

There's only one person to truly hope in, and that's the Lord. He's the Creator of all things and knows every single detail. He's working out His perfect plan even now, and He has an amazing eternity in heaven ready and waiting.

Even on your darkest days, in your worst moments, He's worthy of your hope and your praise. When you see the way He's doing amazing things in your life, be sure to thank Him. Then tell someone else about what He has done!

Father, I'm so glad I can hope in You!
I praise You for the way You work in my life.

A Good Plan

"For I know the plans I have for you," says the Lord, "plans for well-being and not for trouble, to give you a future and a hope."

JEREMIAH 29:11

The Lord has had good plans for the Israelites, His original chosen people, since the Old Testament. Once you trust and believe in Jesus, you're forgiven and accepted into God's family. Now that you're a daughter of God, He looks at you with favor, just as He does His chosen people.

Because you're adopted into God's family, He plans good for your life. He's planning a wonderful future for you; in fact, you can look forward to the coming days and years with hope because of all the amazing plans He has for you.

Even if and when it seems like nothing is working out to any sort of plan, you don't have to fear. Trust that the Lord is doing something truly wonderful!

Lord, it's a relief to know that You already have plans for my future and that they're really, really good. I'm thankful I can put my total trust in You!

Easing a Broken Heart

The Lord is near to those who have a broken heart.
And He saves those who are broken in spirit.

PSALM 34:18

Some people are drawn toward the lonely and brokenhearted. With kindness, they listen quietly and ask caring questions. They don't make the sad person feel worse for needing to cry. They don't scold about tears or pain. They just listen sympathetically.

Even better than a wonderful and truly caring, sympathetic person on earth, the Lord is the ultimate listener and comforter. He's always close to the brokenhearted.

While sad situations may remain sad for a while, God steps in to comfort people who need it. He rescues people who suffer. His kind of rescue might look like a change of circumstances, kindness shared by other people, or unspoken comfort. But He does rescue in amazing ways. Like a breath of fresh air, He steps into hard situations to add comfort and peace.

Lord, it's so comforting to know You're close to the brokenhearted. And You're a rescuer! Please rescue me just when I need You.

A Father's Love

Do not give up when you are punished by God. Be willing to take it, knowing that God is teaching you as a son. Is there a father who does not punish his son sometimes?

HEBREWS 12:7

Not many people appreciate discipline. Getting disciplined by a parent or authority figure usually is uncomfortable, embarrassing, or unwanted. Yet to help you become a better person, that kind of discipline is absolutely necessary.

Similarly, it's not enjoyable to endure the Lord's discipline. When you're out of line and He needs to correct something in your character, He uses difficult situations to correct you. But God chooses to discipline you because you're His daughter and He loves you. If He didn't love you so much, He'd let you go along your own way, without correcting or shaping you into the young woman He'd like you to become.

Lord, I may not like to admit this, but thank You for Your discipline. Thank You for valuing and loving me so much that You correct me for my own good.

Surrounded by His Protection

He answered, "Do not be afraid. For those who are with us are more than those who are with them."
2 KINGS 6:16

The Bible is filled with stories of how God protected His people and worked in their favor in amazing ways. For example, Elisha always knew when enemies planned to attack the Israelites. One night his foes came and surrounded the city where Elisha was staying. When Elisha's servant woke up and saw the enemy troops, he panicked.

But Elisha had no fear. Instead, he knew he was surrounded by the Lord's protection and prayed to the Lord. God answered his prayers, and his enemies never attacked (2 Kings 6:18).

Just as the Lord protected Elisha in a spectacular way, He'll protect you too. You may not be able to see it, but He's protecting you in miraculous ways!

Father, thank You for all the ways You protect me! I'll never know exactly what You do or how You do it, but I'm really glad You do!

A Purpose for Everything

The Lord has made all things for His own plans,
even the sinful for the day of trouble.
PROVERBS 16:4

Some days life seems really random. It's hard to understand why certain things happen and it's almost impossible to connect the dots and figure out how different events could be related to one another.

The great thing with God, though, is that nothing is random. Nothing! He makes everything for a purpose, and He works every single detail together as a part of His plan. He doesn't stick to only the good things. He uses bad things too. He even uses sinful people in different ways.

Instead of getting upset when it seems like evil is triumphing or really awful things happen, relax. God has a reason for all of it. Just because you don't understand what's going on, it doesn't mean He doesn't understand!

Lord, it's amazing that You've made absolutely everything for a purpose. Please help me trust You and wait while You work out Your perfect plan!

Saved by His Life

But God showed His love to us. While we were still sinners, Christ died for us. Now that we have been saved from the punishment of sin by the blood of Christ, He will save us from God's anger also. We hated God. But we were saved from the punishment of sin by the death of Christ. He has brought us back to God and we will be saved by His life.

ROMANS 5:8–10

Have you ever gone out of your way to do something nice for someone else? How much of a sacrifice did you make?

As kind or generous as your sacrifice was, God has given a bigger sacrifice—His only Son. It's not like anyone deserved His kind of gift. In fact, He chose to make that sacrifice when we were sinners and His enemies. Sacrificing your absolutely most prized treasure for your enemy's benefit is more generous, kind, and selfless than anything you've ever experienced.

Lord, I don't deserve Jesus' sacrifice. But I'm thankful for it because of the way it saves me from Your punishment.

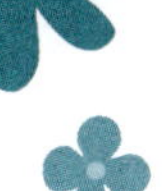

Turning Head Knowledge into Heart Knowledge

May the Lord lead your hearts into the love of God. May He help you as you wait for Christ.

2 THESSALONIANS 3:5

Have you ever heard about the difference between head knowledge and heart knowledge? Head knowledge involves knowing something in your mind; you understand the information. Heart knowledge is different. It changes the way you feel and what you believe.

You may hear about the love of God and feel like you understand it. You've learned about it and have heard that God is love. But has that love actually changed your heart? Do you feel and act differently because of His love?

The Lord can lead your heart into that understanding. He can help you experience Christ's love. Start praying for Him to change your head knowledge into heart knowledge. Then get ready to experience Christ's love in a whole new way!

Father, please help me understand Your love and Your grace with both my head and my heart. I want to know You fully!

Your Good Gifts

O Lord my God, many are the great works You have done, and Your thoughts toward us. No one can compare with You! If I were to speak and tell of them, there would be too many to number.

PSALM 40:5

Have you ever stopped to think about all the great things God has done for you? God doesn't just add a single kind word or thoughtful act to your life. He multiplies them beyond what you could expect or imagine. In fact, He's so generous that none can compare with Him.

When you notice the way God multiplies wonderful things in your life, whether they're His thoughts or His deeds, tell others about what He has done for you! He has done so many great things that you won't remember them all. But for the wonderful things that you do remember, tell someone else. Don't keep His good gifts a secret.

O Lord my God, thank You for multiplying Your great works and Your thoughts toward me! Nothing in this world can compare with You. I praise You for Your greatness!

Reserved

Our body is like a house we live in here on earth. When it is destroyed, we know that God has another body for us in heaven. The new one will not be made by human hands as a house is made. This body will last forever. . . . It is God Who has made us ready for this change. He has given us His Spirit to show us what He has for us.

2 CORINTHIANS 5:1, 5

God is a promise keeper. He has made some pretty amazing promises, and He has kept every single one.

One promise He has made is that He has created a forever home in heaven. While you're here on earth, you'll groan and long for your forever home. Until your moving day, though, God gives you His Holy Spirit as a guarantee. It's like His Spirit reserves your spot until you're there.

The Holy Spirit keeps your future reserved for you while God the Father is working out what He has promised to do!

Father, thank You for preparing a heavenly home for me so I can spend forever with You. Thanks also for giving me Your Spirit as my reservation.

Promise Keeper

"Know then that the Lord your God is God, the faithful God. He keeps His promise and shows His loving-kindness to those who love Him and keep His Laws, even to a thousand family groups in the future."

DEUTERONOMY 7:9

As the Lord looks at a person's heart, He knows who knows Him, believes Him, trusts Him, and obeys Him. He knows who is a true believer. He knows who loves Him deeply.

When you choose to know and love the Lord and keep His commandments, He passes His love on to you too. Choose to live differently than the world out of your love for Him. When you do, He'll be faithful to keep His promises. And His love and favor for you will be beautiful!

Father, I do believe that You are my Lord. I love You! I want to obey You even when it's difficult. Thank You for creating me to have a relationship with You. Thank You for faithfully loving me.

Give All Your Worries

Give all your worries to Him because He cares for you.

1 PETER 5:7

Every single day, you have a lot to think about. Sometimes, especially when you're in the middle of a tough situation, it's easy to focus on all that seems to be going wrong—or all that potentially could go wrong.

Instead of dwelling on the worst, though, you don't have to keep it all bottled up inside. The Lord would love to hear what's troubling you. In fact, He invites you to give Him all your worries and cares.

Why would God want to take all the awful thoughts and feelings you're experiencing? Because He cares for you! He'd love to set you free from all your concerns.

Even if you don't know if you're comfortable sharing all of your problems or burdens with Him, try it. The freedom and peace He'll give you will be worth it!

Lord, being able to give all my worries to You is so freeing. Thank You for caring for me so much!

How Many?

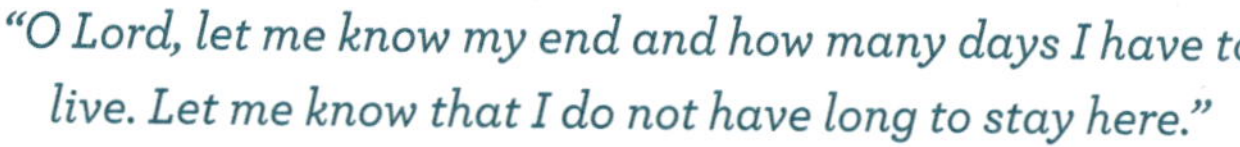

"O Lord, let me know my end and how many days I have to live. Let me know that I do not have long to stay here."

PSALM 39:4

Like it or not, your days are numbered. In fact, before you were born, God knew everything about you, including how many days you'd live.

Even when it can feel like time drags on and on, your time here on earth actually is pretty short. In the big scheme of forever, your days here go by quickly.

If you spend your time focusing on accomplishing a lot or getting more belongings or making more money, it's important to remember that those things that seem so important right now will vanish. So what's the point? If life here on earth is quick, how should you live?

Put your hope in the Lord, and pray that He will help you make the most of every day!

Lord, my hope is in You! Please show me how to live for You all the days of my life.

Before the World Was Made

Even before the world was made, God chose us for Himself because of His love. He planned that we should be holy and without blame as He sees us.

EPHESIANS 1:4

Did you know that God chose you before the world was made? This fact is mind-blowing and an absolute mystery. Long before you chose Him, He chose you. Out of all the people in the world, He chose you to have a relationship with Him.

Can you ever understand the details of how He did this? Or why He did it? No. But the main thing to remember is that He did. And He did it so you can be holy and blameless before Him. You can realize that it's a mystery and thank Him for it!

Father! Thank You for blessing me in Christ with every spiritual blessing! This is something too amazing for me to comprehend, but I'm so thankful for it!

A Rescue

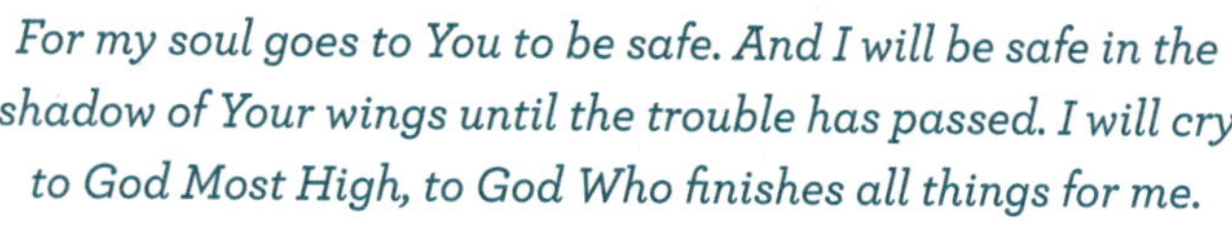

For my soul goes to You to be safe. And I will be safe in the shadow of Your wings until the trouble has passed. I will cry to God Most High, to God Who finishes all things for me.

Psalm 57:1–2

Some days feel like really, really bad days in the terrible, horrible, no good, very bad day way. On your worst days, you don't have to keep all the awful things all to yourself. The Lord wants to know what you feel. He wants you to vent to Him.

You can run to Him for protection. You can cry out to Him for mercy. You can get close to Him and hide yourself in Him. When you go to Him and cry to Him, He'll send help for you. You'll experience His faithful love in a new way as He rescues you.

Father, thank You for Your protection and for being my rescue. I trust You and love You!

The Glow of Dawn

"Because the heart of our God is full of loving-kindness for us, a light from heaven will shine on us. It will give light to those who live in darkness and are under the shadow of death. It will lead our feet in the way of peace."

LUKE 1:78–79

If you've ever gotten up early enough to see the sun rise, you know how the sky is so very dark with the dark of night but starts to lighten right before dawn. All of a sudden, with the sky glowing beautifully, you know you'll see the sun at any moment.

People waited thousands of years for the Messiah to be born, and when He was born, it was like heaven's dawn breaking. The people who were in darkness saw a great light: Jesus!

When Jesus came to this world, He brought the most brilliant, never-ending light to all the darkness!

Jesus, it's so wonderful that You came to save this world. Please guide me in Your way of peace.

Which Path?

Trust in the Lord with all your heart, and do not trust in your own understanding. Agree with Him in all your ways, and He will make your paths straight.

PROVERBS 3:5–6

Decisions can be so difficult, from choosing what outfit you'd like to wear to picking just one flavor of ice cream. But when decisions are bigger than clothing or food, it can be scary and overwhelming to choose just one thing.

Fortunately, the Bible can help your decision-making process. As Proverbs 3:6 points out, the Lord will show you which path to take. He'll point you to the best choice.

How does He do it? You must start out by trusting Him completely. Stop trying to figure things out on your own. Then He'll straighten out your decisions and lead you on the right path.

Father, I'm really thankful You'll lead me when I try to follow You. When I get scared to leave decisions in Your hands, I pray that You'll fill me with courage to obey and follow You. I want to trust in You!

What a Good Choice!

We are to be looking for the great hope and the coming of our great God and the One Who saves, Christ Jesus. He gave Himself for us. He did this by buying us with His blood and making us free from all sin. He gave Himself so His people could be clean and want to do good.

TITUS 2:13–14

When you decide to believe in Jesus, you become part of His family. He saves you, and you belong to Him. Jesus lived and died as a perfect sacrifice for you so you would be free from sin and from wanting to live for the things of this world.

Through His power, every time you choose to do what is right in His eyes, you show yourself and the people around you that you're His own. Your right choices show that you're waiting for Him! When you live the way He likes, you're quick to choose what's good and stay away from sin.

Jesus, thank You for rescuing me.
Please help me live a right life for You!

Better Than Life

My lips will praise You because Your loving-kindness is better than life.

Psalm 63:3

One of the easiest Bible verses to remember is part of 1 John 4:16: "God is love." God *is* love, and the Bible says that His love is better than life. But what about His love is better than life?

You are loved by God with a love that will never move or change. His love for you is faithfully and firmly fixed in place. His love doesn't depend on what you're feeling. It's dependable. It's better than life.

Because you're so completely loved with a love that will never change, the right response is to praise Him! Praise Him for His goodness and His amazing love. Thank Him for choosing to love you. And tell someone else about it!

Father, I praise You! Your steadfast love is better than life, and I'm completely thrilled that I get to experience it.

My Rock

So the Lord God says, "See, I lay in Jerusalem a Stone of great worth to build upon, a tested Stone. Anyone who puts his trust in Him will not be afraid of what will happen."

ISAIAH 28:16

All throughout the Bible, Jesus is described as a rock. He's the foundation of the church, and He can become the foundation of your life. A foundation for a building needs to be strong. If it's a cracked or crumbling foundation, the entire building will collapse into a heap of rubble.

Jesus, as a foundation, is rock solid. If you choose to build your life on Him, you'll never be shaken. You won't be disturbed. You won't crumble and fall.

Instead, with a life built on the rock of Jesus, you'll stand strong, even in the storms of life. Like strong, ancient buildings that still stand today, you'll remain even when it seems like everything else around you crumbles.

Lord Jesus, I'm so thankful You're a strong foundation! When I build my life on You and obey Your Word, I don't have to fear.

In His Shadow

For You have been my help. And I sing for joy in the shadow of Your wings.

Psalm 63:7

Think about shadows for a minute. Shadows provide cooling shade in the heat of the day. They are silhouettes of objects and not the objects themselves. You need to be fairly close to whatever object is creating the shadow to see the shadow. If you're standing outside on a sunny day, your own shadow looks like it could be connected to you.

When you choose to live close to the Lord by following Him, He will help you. In fact, you can be kept safe in the shadow of His wings.

Just like a bird keeps its babies safe under its wings, God will do the same for you! He'll hide you there and keep you safe. And under the shadow of His wings, you can sing for joy.

Father, thank You for helping me! Because You love me with an everlasting love, I pray I'll take comfort in the shadow of Your wings.

New and Improved

Put away the old person you used to be. Have nothing to do with your old sinful life. It was sinful because of being fooled into following bad desires. Let your minds and hearts be made new.

EPHESIANS 4:22–23

Everyone has a life before Christ. Even if you're introduced to Jesus when you're young, you still have a life before and after you give your life to Christ. Other people live long lives and never come to know Him. They might hear about Him but never commit their lives to Him.

When you choose to answer Christ's invitation to join God's family (you can do this right now by telling Him you believe in Him and want to follow Him), things will totally change. He will make you new. Not only will all your sins be forgiven, but He will also guide and direct you. You can get rid of your old way of living and trade it for a new and improved life.

Father, thanks for offering me a new, better life through Jesus. I'm glad I don't have to stay trapped in my old way of living. You choose me, and I accept Your invitation to come into Your family!

Clingworthy

My soul holds on to You. Your right hand holds me up.

Psalm 63:8

When you were younger, do you remember clinging to someone you trusted? Whoever it might have been, think about what it felt like to cling to them. You didn't want to let go, right? With all of your strength, you wrapped your body around them in such a way that you were stuck on tight.

Now that you're older, you may not cling to many people for love or protection. But you can use that same clinging action to hold on to the Lord. Just like when you were young and clingy, your soul can wrap around God and hold on tight. Don't let go!

Why would you want to be stuck so close to God? He loves you totally and completely. He wants what's best for you. And He holds you up every day of your life. If anyone is clingworthy, it's our Lord!

Father, I want to cling to You! I trust You completely, and I'm thankful for Your love.

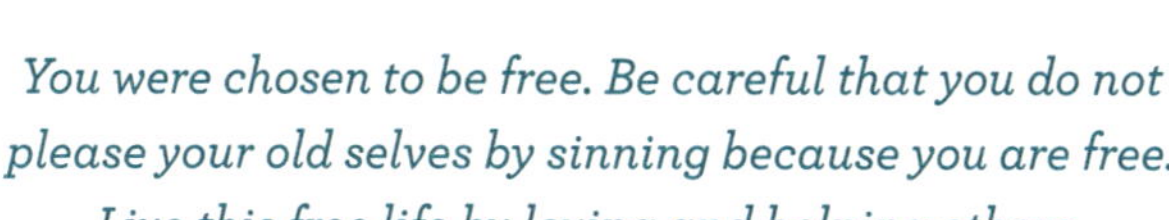

A Life of Freedom

You were chosen to be free. Be careful that you do not please your old selves by sinning because you are free. Live this free life by loving and helping others.

GALATIANS 5:13

Freedom seems like such an important gift. Everyone wants to be free—free to do or say or think however they choose.

Apart from Christ, you're a prisoner and slave. You can't help the fact that you're shackled to your sinful way of life. But in Christ? You have freedom! You're free from the bondage of your sins.

If and when you commit your life to Christ, use your freedom to live a life of love! Step out in faith to love the unlovable of this world. Help other people. Loving others with kindness and thoughtfulness and mercy is a fantastic way to live out your life of freedom in Christ.

Lord Jesus, You lived a life of love when You were here on earth. I want to be just like You! Please help me use my freedom in You to love others well.

His People

Know that the Lord is God. It is He Who made us, and not we ourselves. We are His people and the sheep of His field.

Psalm 100:3

Think of a time when you felt left out of something. It hurt, didn't it? It's never any fun to feel excluded or like you're not part of a group.

The great news is that once you believe in the Lord, you're part of His group. He has called you to be part of His people. You're included in His favorites. He doesn't exclude you.

And how do you become part of His people? This isn't something you're naturally born into, and it's not anything you earn. Instead, God must choose you. He wants you to be part of His family. But to be part of His family, you need to reach a point where you trust Him enough to commit your life to Him.

Once you're part of God's family, enjoy it! You're His people. He made you, and you are His.

Father, thank You for including me in Your family. I am so grateful to be Your child.

Lifted Up and Carried

He suffered with them in all their troubles, and the angel of the Lord saved them. In His loving-kindness He paid the price and made them free. He lifted them up and carried them all the days of long ago.

ISAIAH 63:9

If you've spent all day working hard, your body will feel very tired. Maybe you've hiked for miles or spent an entire day working with your family. Or maybe your brain is exhausted after studying hard or thinking through some troubling situations.

You might actually feel so tired and worn out that you wish someone would pick you up and carry you. The amazing news is that you can let go and collapse into the arms of your loving heavenly Father. He will lift you up when you're weak and will carry you. He knows when you're going through troubles, and because He loves you, He is ready and willing to help.

Father, what a relief You are for me! In Your love and mercy, You'll help me through my toughest situations. You'll even lift me up and carry me when I need You the most.

Bigger Plans

God is a God of peace. He raised our Lord Jesus from the dead. . . . May God give you every good thing you need so you can do what He wants. May He do in us what pleases Him through Jesus Christ.

Hebrews 13:20–21

God does truly amazing things! He brought Jesus back to life after He was dead for three days. He faithfully leads those who believe in Him. And He has given promises that will last forever.

Just as He can do unthinkably huge things in this world, He also gives you everything you need so you can do His will. That means He takes care of every detail, and He gives you everything good so you can do His work. Nothing will stop Him from working in you to do what is pleasing to Him. He has bigger plans for you, and He's giving you everything you need to do those plans!

Father, help me understand Your plans for me. I want to trust You completely as You get me ready for Your good work. Thank You for working in this world and in my life!

What's the Plan?

The mind of a man plans his way,
but the Lord shows him what to do.
PROVERBS 16:9

You know what you'd like to do. You might know when you'd love to do it. You even might try to detail every little step to reach your goals.

Dreaming and hoping and planning aren't bad. But just because you plan how you'd like something to work out doesn't mean it will. In fact, there's a good chance your plans just won't work out. And that's okay.

As you think about your present and your future, keep dreaming. Keep thinking about what you'd like to do in your life and with your life. But as you do this, remember the Lord is the one who will establish your steps. He's the one who will make your plans into reality in His own timing and in His own way.

As you trust Him with your plans, He'll surprise you with a future that's better than you can ever imagine.

Father, please help me relax and trust You completely with my future! Please guide my plans too.

Known

The truth of God cannot be changed. It says, "The Lord knows those who are His." And, "Everyone who says he is a Christian must turn away from sin!"

2 TIMOTHY 2:19

Think about your treasured possessions. What are they? And why are they so special to you? Are they meaningful because of certain memories? Did someone give you these items? Did you find something in an unusual way or at a unique location?

Just as you know your treasured possessions and what makes them so meaningful to you, the Lord knows you too. To Him, you are a treasured possession. He paid a great cost for you—His Son's life—and that makes you really important to Him.

As you confess the name of the Lord and turn to Him, He delights in you. He knows you are His, and He loves and adores you.

Father, it's so very good to be known by You! I confess that You are Lord. I praise You for Your goodness and thank You for Your never-ending faithfulness.

My Fortress

My soul is quiet and waits for God alone. My hope comes from Him. He alone is my rock and the One Who saves me. He is my strong place. I will not be shaken.

Psalm 62:5–6

If you've ever seen a castle, think about how it's surrounded by a fortress. If the gates to the fortress are closed, there's no way in. You can't climb the walls or even push your way in. A strong fortress creates a safe, secure place.

Just like physical fortresses defend, the Lord is your fortress. He protects you. Through Him, you're safe. With Him on your side, you won't be shaken, even when enemies attack and you feel like you're in the middle of a battle.

Because the Lord is your strong defense, you don't have to worry. In fact, you can rest in Him—not just relax and let down your guard, but truly rest. He's your strong place. He's your protection. He's your fortress.

Lord, thank You for being my safe place and my protection! I wouldn't want anything or anyone else to be my fortress.

Stronger

I pray that God's great power will make you strong,
and that you will have joy as you wait and do not give up.
Colossians 1:11

Some activities or friendships feel so draining. As much as you invest time and energy into them, they leave you feeling zapped. Instead of feeling energized and full of joy, you feel used up and worn out.

Your relationship with God is not like that. In fact, He gives strength with all of His glorious power, and He fills you with joy. There's no lack of energy with Him—He fills you up so you feel alive!

As He strengthens you with His own power, you're able to use it to endure patiently. Even when you face energy-zapping situations, His power will give you strength to endure, along with a healthy dose of His joy. He'll add pep to your step.

Thank You, Lord, for Your strength!
It's amazing to be filled with Your power and joy.
Thank You! Sometimes I really need it to keep going.

Knowing and Understanding

I pray that the great God and Father of our Lord Jesus Christ may give you the wisdom of His Spirit. . . . I pray that your hearts will be able to understand. I pray that you will know about the hope given by God's call. I pray that you will see how great the things are that He has promised to those who belong to Him.

EPHESIANS 1:17–18

When you first believe in Christ, it's the beginning of a journey that will last the rest of your life. Over time, you'll get to know Him and become more like Him.

The good news is that you don't have to worry about this process. You're not left alone to figure it out on your own. The Lord can and will give you spiritual wisdom. As He does, you'll understand more and more about what He has promised!

Father, I'm so relieved that I don't have to figure out spiritual details on my own. Please fill me with Your wisdom and insight so I can learn more about You—and who I am in You.

Forever Love

But the loving-kindness of the Lord is forever and forever on those who fear Him. And what is right with God is given forever to their children's children.

PSALM 103:17

Forever is a long, long time! It's hard to understand the way forever never begins or ends but always, always exists.

God has promised that He loves you forever. His love for you will go on and on and on. He'll never stop loving you. In fact, He loves you so much that His love and favor for you eventually will even spill out onto your children and grandchildren.

This kind of love isn't for every person on the planet. Sadly, some people don't want His love. And because of their choice, they won't get it. But as you fear Him and respect Him as the Lord of lords, He'll always and forever wow you with the amazing love He has for you.

Father, Your love for me is pretty amazing. I'm blown away by the fact that it will never end. Thank You! I love You too!

No Reason

He is the One Who saved us from the punishment of sin. He is the One Who chose us to do His work. It is not because of anything we have done. But it was His plan from the beginning that He would give us His loving-favor through Christ Jesus.

2 TIMOTHY 1:9

Have you ever been chosen for something just because? It didn't matter what you did or didn't do, but you received some sort of favor or gift anyway.

Your relationship with Jesus is like that. It doesn't matter who you are or what you've done. If He has called you to Himself, it's because He chose you. It's not because of what you have or haven't done. He chose you for His very own purpose before the beginning of time. Wow!

Thank You! Thank You for thinking of me and saving me and having a plan for my life even before the beginning of time. Please help me live the sort of life You would have me live. I want to live for You!

Praise Him!

Praise the Lord, all nations!
Praise Him, all people! For His loving-kindness
toward us is great. And the truth of the
Lord lasts forever. Praise the Lord!

PSALM 117:1–2

When you think about all the Lord has done for you, it seems only natural to praise Him. He's worthy of your praise. He's deserving of it. He loves you with a powerful, never-ending, never-stopping love. He's forever faithful. That's worthy of praise!

When you look around and see all that God has done and is doing, a right response is to praise Him. Does His creation take your breath away? Praise Him! Do you stand amazed at the way He works out tiny details? Praise Him! When you think of what you deserve because of the way you have sometimes disappointed Him by your disobedience, yet how He heaps blessing after blessing on you, praise Him! The Lord is great. And He's greatly to be praised.

Lord God, I praise You! I praise You for being Lord of all. I praise You for being so great yet taking notice of me.

Approaching God's Throne

Let us go with complete trust to the throne of God. We will receive His loving-kindness and have His loving-favor to help us whenever we need it.

HEBREWS 4:16

Imagine the throne of a king, crafted with gold, velvet, and jewels. Just by seeing that throne, you'd know you were in the presence of royalty. And if you saw a king sitting on his throne? You'd feel humbled and awkward as you tried to decide whether to bow or curtsy.

If you'd approach an earthly king and his throne like this, it would feel completely humbling and terrifying to approach the throne of the King of kings. Yet the Bible says we can approach God's throne of grace with confidence. Say what? Confidence instead of trembling and dread?

When you approach God's throne, He'll give you kindness and favor. He'll help you when you need Him the most. Instead of shaking with fear, you can confidently come toward Him, knowing that He loves you and wants to help you.

Father, I worship You as King of kings.

Lasting

Give thanks to the Lord, for He is good.
His loving-kindness lasts forever.
PSALM 118:1

What are some things that last a really long time? Antique furniture? Ancient buildings?

God's love for you lasts so much longer than any of those things. In fact, His love for you lasts forever! His love endures in a lasting way because it's durable and can withstand anything. His love is patient. It's solid. It's not going to give in.

Give thanks to the Lord because His love is so reliable, so enduring, and because it lasts forever. Because the Lord is good, it's worth thanking Him too! He could be unkind or unloving, but He is goodness. He is love. And because He chooses to treat you with His goodness and love, it's only natural to thank Him. Instead of taking Him for granted, be grateful to be loved by Him!

Thank You, Father, for being so good to me.
It's such a gift to be loved by You.

A Place to Belong

"There are many rooms in My Father's house. If it were not so, I would have told you. I am going away to make a place for you. After I go and make a place for you, I will come back and take you with Me. Then you may be where I am."

JOHN 14:2–3

Knowing where you'll live for a long time is a huge comfort. You can settle in and feel at home.

Right now, Jesus is preparing a place for you to live. While He knows where you'll stay tonight and any other night of your life on earth, those aren't the homes He's preparing for you. As long as you choose to follow Him, He's preparing a place for you after your life here on earth is over. He's fixing a room just for you in His Father's house—in heaven! You'll belong with Him!

Lord Jesus, it's a huge comfort to know You're preparing a place for me even right now. Thank You!

No Worries!

"I tell you this: Do not worry about your life. Do not worry about what you are going to eat and drink. Do not worry about what you are going to wear. Is not life more important than food? Is not the body more important than clothes?"

MATTHEW 6:25

When was the last time you wondered about what you'd eat for breakfast? Or what clothes you'd like to wear?

It can be really natural to think about meals and outfits, and sometimes it's tempting to worry about them. But Jesus taught that you don't have to worry about things like food or clothing. Why not? Because your body is worth more than clothing. Your life is worth way more than food.

When you think about who you are, deep down, you're so much more than the things you put inside or outside your body. The Lord knows what you need, and He'll faithfully provide it for you. You don't have to worry about it!

Father, thank You for providing everything I could ever need!

Death to Life

But God had so much loving-kindness. He loved us with such a great love. Even when we were dead because of our sins, He made us alive by what Christ did for us. You have been saved from the punishment of sin by His loving-favor.

EPHESIANS 2:4–5

Being separated from someone because of death hurts. God knows that, and it never was part of His original plan. Sin brought death and separation into God's perfect world.

God hated death so much—and He loved you so very much—that He made a way to get rid of the separation that death brings. He sent Jesus to this world to live a perfect life and die so He could conquer death, rise from the dead, and live forever.

Since Jesus did that, everyone who trusts in Him and His resurrected life will experience the same life after death. Through His great love and kindness, God makes you alive with Christ!

Father, I could never save myself, and I know it. But You sent Jesus so that I could be made alive after death. Thank You!

Wonderfully Made

For You made the parts inside me. You put me together inside my mother. I will give thanks to You, for the greatness of the way I was made brings fear. Your works are great and my soul knows it very well.

PSALM 139:13–14

Do you realize there's nothing accidental about you? You were formed *on* purpose *with* a purpose. God formed you—all of you. He had a plan for you and your life, and then He put you together wonderfully.

Sometimes you might not feel wonderful. It might seem easy to focus on your flaws. But your feelings don't change facts.

What actually is true is that the Lord did make you in a wonderful way. The God of the universe chose to make you just the way He did. Trust that He did a great thing. When you find yourself doubting the way you've been made, ask Him to help you realize the truth and see yourself the way He sees you.

Father, sometimes I have a really hard time believing You made me in a wonderful way. Please help me find my worth in You rather than in my forever-changing feelings.

Changing

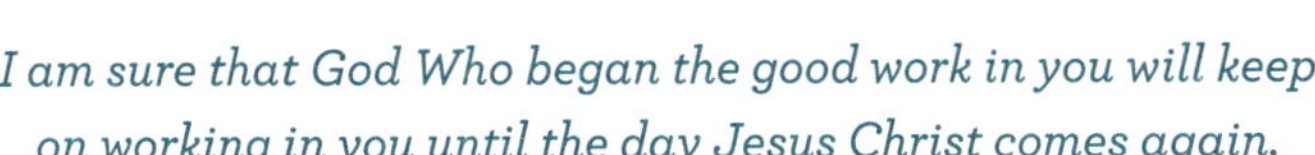

I am sure that God Who began the good work in you will keep on working in you until the day Jesus Christ comes again.

PHILIPPIANS 1:6

How patient are you with yourself? When you know you should change or improve something, do you feel frustrated or annoyed that you haven't already changed?

Hold on. Take a deep breath. One really important fact to remember is that you can't do absolutely everything in the world perfectly and immediately know how to do it. You will grow and change. You'll learn and keep learning and practicing more and more.

Whether you realize it or not, the Lord began a good work in you. He's not going to let that good work remain unfinished. Instead, He'll keep working on you every day of your life. If you let Him do His good work in you, you'll change and improve until you become just who He wants you to be.

Father, please help me to be more patient with myself and Your process! I don't like my imperfections. I'm really impatient. Please help me learn to wait on You.

Not Alone

You are my hiding place. You keep me safe from trouble. All around me are Your songs of being made free.

PSALM 32:7

If you're going through a difficult time, it's easy to feel discouraged and down. But even when you face your darkest days, you're not alone.

If you run to God, He can be your hiding place. He'll be your protection. In fact, He's right here, surrounding you. Knowing you're not alone can be a huge comfort.

So how can you notice a difference, even when it seems like you're in the middle of trouble? Pray to God! Tell Him everything you're going through and how it makes you feel. Tell Him what you wish would happen. Then ask Him for His help. Ask Him to give you peace and direction. Once you've done that, He'll make a difference.

Father, it feels so good to know that I'm never alone. You are my hiding place! Thank You for surrounding me with protection. I want to rely on You.

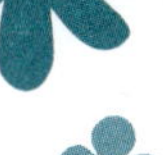

Amazing Gifts

God raised us up from death when He raised up Christ Jesus. He has given us a place with Christ in the heavens. He did this to show us through all the time to come the great riches of His loving-favor. He has shown us His kindness through Christ Jesus.

EPHESIANS 2:6–7

Once you believe in Christ, all sorts of wonderful things happen. You're promised to be resurrected like Him, from death to life. When you eventually die, you'll be with Him in heaven. Both of these things are pretty amazing!

You'll never be able to compare anything with how priceless these gifts are. They're riches given to you out of God's love and favor. Out of His kindness, He gives you an undeserved gift of forever life with Him.

Father, thank You for promising me so much through Jesus! Nothing on this earth can compare with the riches You have stored up for me. You are so kind and over-the-top generous. Thank You!

Hide-and-Seek

"He made from one blood all nations who live on the earth. He set the times and places where they should live. They were to look for God. Then they might feel after Him and find Him because He is not far from each one of us."

ACTS 17:26–27

When you've played hide-and-seek, has there ever been a time when you couldn't find a hider? As much as you tried seeking, did someone stay hidden until you gave up?

While some people like finding a great hiding spot, God is not like that. In fact, God gives people the desire to seek Him, and then He tries to make it obvious where He can be found. It's like He gives all kinds of hints and clues, so if you'd just put them all together, you would find Him really easily.

God is not far away. And He's not trying to stay hidden. He wants you to find Him!

Father, I'm glad You want people to find You! Please make Yourself absolutely clear to me.

Never Returned

"All whom My Father has given to Me will come to Me. I will never turn away anyone who comes to Me. . . . The Father sent Me. He did not want Me to lose any of all those He gave Me. He wants Me to raise them to life on the last day."

JOHN 6:37, 39

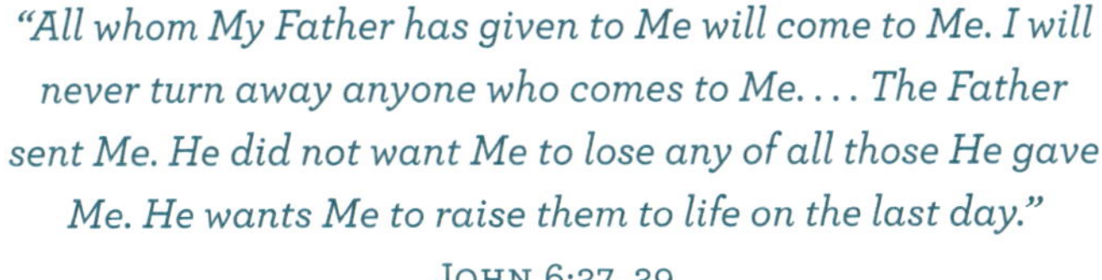

Most stores have return policies. If you've made a purchase, typically you can return items for your money back. There are no returns with God. He won't spend the precious blood of Jesus for you and then change His mind.

Jesus promised that if you come to Him in faith, He will never, ever reject you. And God the Father made sure that Jesus wouldn't lose you—not by choice, not by accident. Every single person who puts their trust in Christ for salvation will be raised up on the last day. That means you'll never be returned.

Father, thank You for choosing to accept me. Knowing that You won't change Your mind is such an unbelievable comfort.

Real Love

God has chosen you. You are holy and loved by Him. . . .
You should be kind to others and have no pride. Be gentle and be willing to wait for others. Try to understand other people. Forgive each other. If you have something against someone, forgive him. That is the way the Lord forgave you. And to all these things, you must add love. Love holds everything and everybody together and makes all these good things perfect.

COLOSSIANS 3:12–14

People in this world talk about loving and treating others with kindness, but do they really show love? Are their words and actions very kind?

God calls you to live a holy life filled with real, sincere love. Let your love shine through your kindness. Be patient and gentle with others and with yourself. Humbly remember who you are, and forgive others. When you live like that, you'll show the world what real love and kindness are all about.

Father, I love You! I want to obey You! Please help me show others Your love and kindness.

Perfect Peace

"Peace I leave with you. My peace I give to you.
I do not give peace to you as the world gives.
Do not let your hearts be troubled or afraid."

JOHN 14:27

Peace is something that sounds so wonderful. But even as it sounds wonderful, it also seems fairly impossible. What would actual peace look like? Are people actually willing to step aside from their own pride? Can people willingly let disagreements go?

Jesus knew the world promoted a different peace than He offered. He knew that when people dealt with disagreements, worldly peace wasn't possible. But through Him, peace isn't just possible; it is promised.

Jesus is in the habit of giving peace to those who love Him and rely on Him. He'll flood your heart with peace in a way that nothing else can. He gives the gift of perfect peace because perfect peace is a part of Him. And He offers it to you.

Lord Jesus, I want Your peace!
Thank You for not giving as the world gives.
Thank You for Your wonderful gift of peace.

Every Moment

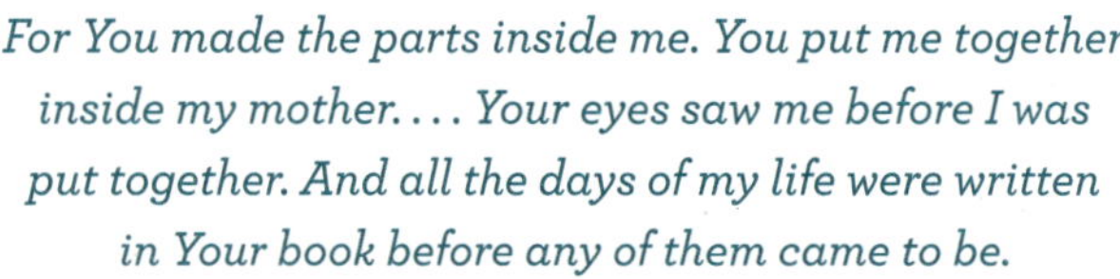

For You made the parts inside me. You put me together inside my mother. . . . Your eyes saw me before I was put together. And all the days of my life were written in Your book before any of them came to be.

Psalm 139:13, 16

The Lord made you in an amazing way, but He didn't stop at creating your body or your personality. He went on to know every day of your life. He knows every moment that you've had and every moment you will ever have.

Even as God knows everything about you, He still chooses to love you. He chose to call you to Himself. He didn't see every day of your life and give up on you. He didn't create you to be just the way you are and push you aside. No, He knows you completely and still loves you.

Father, I don't understand how You know every single part of me and still choose to love me, but I'm so glad You do! Thank You for creating and choosing me.

A Praying Friend

I ask God that you may know what He wants you to do. I ask God to fill you with the wisdom and understanding the Holy Spirit gives. Then your lives will please the Lord. You will do every kind of good work, and you will know more about God.

COLOSSIANS 1:9–10

Think about someone you care about very much. You want the best for that person, right? You'd be happy to see that person receive good things.

That's exactly what the apostle Paul was talking about when he wrote a letter to his friends in Colossae. Paul prayed for his friends all the time. And he prayed for the Lord to bless them in big ways. Paul knew that by praying, his friends would be able to understand how best to know and please the Lord. Once they did that, their lives also would produce all sorts of wonderful outcomes.

How can you start praying for your friends?

Father, please give my friends and me spiritual wisdom and understanding so we can know You better and better.

Where's Your Trust?

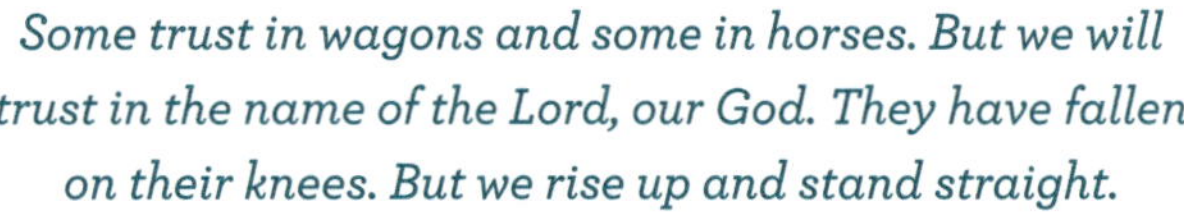

Some trust in wagons and some in horses. But we will trust in the name of the Lord, our God. They have fallen on their knees. But we rise up and stand straight.

PSALM 20:7–8

Where do you place your trust? Does owning a lot of belongings make you feel safe? Do you feel better about yourself if you have a bunch of friends? Do you trust in your own talents?

It's easy to look to other things to make us feel safe and comfortable. But none of those things are worthy of your trust. In fact, all of those things will fail you. It's not a matter of *if* they'll fail you but *when* they will.

There's one who is always trustworthy and who will never fail. That one is the Lord our God. When you trust in Him, you won't be disappointed. Instead, you'll rise up and stand firm in His strength.

Father, I praise You for being worthy of my trust. Forgive me for the times when I look to other things besides You. I want to turn to You alone!

The Gift of Grace

For by His loving-favor you have been saved from the punishment of sin through faith. It is not by anything you have done. It is a gift of God. It is not given to you because you worked for it. If you could work for it, you would be proud.

EPHESIANS 2:8–9

Grace sounds like a perfect word to use at church: "Amazing grace! How sweet the sound!"

But what exactly does *grace* mean? And what does it mean to be saved by it? Simply put, grace is an undeserved gift, a special favor of mercy, or an act of kindness.

Your faith in Christ alone saves you. There's absolutely nothing in the world you can do to save yourself. There's no amount of talent or good works or money or status that can save you. The only thing that can and does save you is the grace of God. Your faith opens up God's gift of grace to you.

Father, I don't deserve Your grace or Your forgiveness or Your favor. But You've kindly and generously given them to me anyway. Thank You!

Forever and Ever

Lord, You have been the place of comfort for all people of all time. Before the mountains were born, before You gave birth to the earth and the world, forever and ever, You are God.

PSALM 90:1–2

Forever is such a hard concept to wrap your mind around, yet God always has been God. He is God now. And He always will be God. There never is a moment in forever when He's not God.

We can try to figure out the reality of forever until our heads hurt. We also can learn to appreciate the fact that there are some things in life we'll never truly understand or comprehend. Eternity is just one of those things. But we can choose to believe it by faith and thank God for the way He comforts us like nothing and no one else.

Father, I praise You. You are infinitely more than I can comprehend, but You are God.

His Own Image

And God made man in His own likeness. In the likeness of God He made him. He made both male and female.

GENESIS 1:27

In the beginning, God created absolutely everything. Once there had been nothing but God, and then He created everything. And it was good.

God created every living thing, but when it came to humans, He did something very different. He created men and women in His own image. No other living creatures in all creation were made in God's own image—just humans.

Because God created you in His own image, that makes you an image bearer. You bear the Lord's image. Every single person, living or dead, is made in His image. And every single person matters to God. Not every single person will choose to spend eternity with Him, but He still calls to every single one in His own special way.

Father, I'll never understand why You created humans in Your own image, but I'm honored that You did. I pray that I'd live a life worthy of an image bearer!

Show Me the Way

Let me hear Your loving-kindness in the morning, for I trust in You. Teach me the way I should go for I lift up my soul to You.

PSALM 143:8

Life is confusing. Sometimes it makes sense and you're confident of what you should do. But other times? Totally uncertain.

Instead of feeling lost in confusion, trying to muddle through life on your own, you can ask the Lord for guidance. Like the psalmist, when you feel uncertain, simply ask God, "Show me the way I should go!"

Like a shepherd, the Lord will faithfully and gently lead you. He has promised never to leave you. And He'll never forsake you. Instead, when you entrust your life to Him and belong to Him, He will guide you by His unfailing, never-ending love.

Father, it's such a relief to know that You love me so much that I can trust You. Please show me the way I should go!

His!

"See, heaven and the highest heavens, the earth and all that is in it belong to the Lord your God."
DEUTERONOMY 10:14

If you create an art project, it's all yours, right? You've poured your creativity into it; you've spent time forming it and perfecting it. When you've finished your creation, you're free to do whatever you please with it, whether it means displaying it proudly, setting it aside, or giving it away as a gift.

Similarly, what God made belongs to Him. As the Creator of absolutely everything, He can look with ownership then decide what He'd like to do.

Since He is God, His ways are higher than your ways and His thoughts are higher than your thoughts. He can and will make the best decisions. When you realize this truth, you can take the time to praise Him. He has created everything! That's amazing! And everything belongs to Him! He's worthy of your praise!

Father, I praise You for Your power and might. I stand in awe of Your creative creation. I'm so glad I belong to You.

From Weak to Strong

He gives strength to the weak. And He gives power to him who has little strength. Even very young men get tired and become weak and strong young men trip and fall. But they who wait upon the Lord will get new strength.

Isaiah 40:29–31

Ever wish you had an extra burst of strength? Maybe you're exhausted after physical activity. Or maybe, after a really tough test, your brain seems completely wiped out. Whenever you work really hard, you naturally feel worn out.

Even when you're exhausted, you don't have to give up. If you wait for the Lord, He'll help by strengthening you. This extra boost of energy won't happen automatically. But when you need to feel energized and refreshed, ask the Lord for strength and energy. Wait for Him, step out in faith, and watch what He'll do through you.

Father, thank You for caring so much about me that You'll actually give me energy and strength! I'm so glad I can rely on You.

Helping Others in Love

"For sure, I tell you, whoever gives you a cup of water to drink in My name because you belong to Christ will not lose his reward from God."

MARK 9:41

Jesus taught that His followers would be known by their love, but sometimes it can seem tricky to show love to someone else. (Especially if you feel awkward and aren't exactly sure what to say or do!)

Many times you don't have to go out of your way in an outrageous way to show Jesus' love. It might be as simple as helping out with a task. Or you could invite the lonely to be a part of something—maybe you could get to know your neighbor a little better or could invite a new girl to sit with you at lunch.

Watch for people who seem to need help, then bravely step up, get to know them, and see if you can help out in any way. You might be surprised by how God will use you!

Father, please help me realize when people need help, and please help me figure out ways to help them.

Now and Later

For sure, You will give me goodness and loving-kindness all the days of my life. Then I will live with You in Your house forever.

PSALM 23:6

Choosing to trust and follow the Lord is a win-win situation for you, both now and later. For now, His love and goodness will follow you not just today or tomorrow but all the days of your life. Every one!

As if that's not a huge enough blessing, God has created a forever home for you. You'll get to dwell there—not just visit. You can move in and settle down and be with Him. If you think you have experienced His goodness and love here on earth, just wait until you're spending eternity with Him in His house!

Father, thank You for loving me and being so good to me now. And thank You for inviting me to stay with You in Your home forever!

Pray First

If you do not have wisdom, ask God for it. He is always ready to give it to you and will never say you are wrong for asking. You must have faith as you ask Him. You must not doubt. Anyone who doubts is like a wave which is pushed around by the sea.

JAMES 1:5–6

Sometimes life seems confusing. It's hard to know what's right or wrong. And other times, when it's time to make a big decision, so many answers seem like they might possibly be good. But is there one right choice? Or are they all right choices?

When life feels confusing and you truly don't know what to do, know that you're not alone in your decision-making. The Lord loves when you seek wisdom. Simply ask Him in faith, believing He can and will answer you. Trust Him to guide you, and then step out in faith. Sometimes He'll answer you loud and clear, and other times He'll lead you in quiet trust.

Father, no matter how You lead me, I'm thankful You do lead me. Please guide me! I'd love to make a wise choice!

Give Me Some Shelter

He who lives in the safe place of the Most High will be in the shadow of the All-powerful. I will say to the Lord, "You are my safe and strong place, my God, in Whom I trust."

PSALM 91:1–2

When you're outside, you're either under shelter or you're not. If a rainstorm suddenly begins, you'll know right away if you're under the protection of a shelter. Shelters do a fantastic job of protecting people from the elements of nature, whether it's the blazing sun, pouring rain, blustery wind, or freezing snow.

Just as you need physical shelter for your long-term safety and short-term comfort, spiritual shelter is essential too. When you trust in the Lord, you decide you'd like Him to be your safe place. He becomes your safe, strong place. You can rest in His shadow. You can find protection in His shelter.

Father, in the storms of life, I really need Your shelter. Thank You for protecting me and comforting me. Lord, I trust in You!

Highway of Holiness

And a road will be there. It will be called the Holy Way. Those who are unclean will not travel on it. But it will be for those who walk in that way. Fools will not walk on it. . . . But those whose sin has been paid for will walk there.

Isaiah 35:8–9

When you follow the Lord, you're set apart from people who choose not to follow Him. And as you start to follow Him, it's as if He sets you on the Highway of Holiness, or the Holy Way.

Holy living means you're set apart for God. You won't do much of what the world does because you're walking with God now and not the world. You're His and not the world's.

Others around you will focus on the world's values and beliefs and current trends, but they're missing out on what's lasting and true. Instead of being pulled off God's highway, keep your eyes fixed on Him!

Father, please help me follow You faithfully! I don't want to be tempted by the cares and desires of this world.

New and Improved

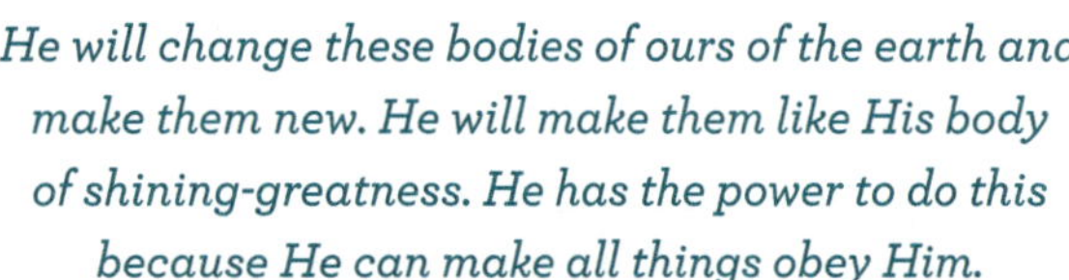

He will change these bodies of ours of the earth and make them new. He will make them like His body of shining-greatness. He has the power to do this because He can make all things obey Him.

PHILIPPIANS 3:21

Have you ever wished you could change something about yourself? Maybe you're not completely pleased with the way you look. Or maybe it seems tough to appreciate your body.

Your body won't stay this same way forever. Sure, you'll grow and change. Your height might stay close to the same, and you'll gain and lose weight. Even with those differences, your body will completely change once you die. The Lord will take the body you have now and change it into a new body. Your new, immortal body will last forever.

How will this happen? God will change your body into an everlasting one with His power. All you'll need to do is watch it all happen!

Father, it's a little surprising to think of You transforming my body into something new. However You'll do it, I know it will be amazing!

Secrets Revealed

"The secret things belong to the Lord our God. But the things that are made known belong to us and to our children forever, so we may obey all the words of this Law."

DEUTERONOMY 29:29

When the Lord set apart the Israelites, He gave His law to guide them. The Israelites knew the Lord chose to reveal His law to them. They knew they were supposed to live by His law, obey it, then pass on the truth and instruction to their children. Yet in their human nature, it became easy to slip away from the commandments and disobey.

God continued to call the Israelites back from their sin. He knew that as imperfect, sinful people, the Israelites could never keep the law perfectly in their own power. He also knew that His Son, Jesus, could change everything by fulfilling the law. So He sent His Son into the world to be the Savior, not just of the Israelites but of all who believe in Him and call on His name. That includes you!

Father, thank You for revealing Your Son to me. I pray that He'll transform my heart.

Filled with Joy

The Lord has done great things for us and we are glad.

Psalm 126:3

Take a minute to think of all the great things the Lord has done for you. What special people has He brought into your life? What are some of your favorite things in life—like your favorite foods? Favorite hobbies? Favorite songs? Favorite ways to spend time with your friends? Favorite animals? Favorite places?

All of those favorite things are really great, and each one is a good gift to you from God. When He brings such good things into your life, whether it's a hysterically funny conversation with a friend, a delicious home-cooked meal, or an amazing day, enjoy all the joy you feel. As you're filled with joy, be sure to thank God. He has done great things for you, and He's worthy of your thanks and praise!

Father, thank You so much for all the good things You do for me. You know how happy I am when I experience my favorite people and things.

Uniquely You

We are His work. He has made us to belong to Christ Jesus so we can work for Him. He planned that we should do this.

EPHESIANS 2:10

When God created you, He gave you a unique set of gifts and strengths and talents that no one else in the world has or ever will have. You're uniquely you! He has created you in this most special way for His own special purpose.

He didn't form you to keep all your talents hidden away for yourself. He crafted you to be you so you could share your gifts with others. He even created you to do good works—and He has prepared those good works for you already.

You already have the talents and abilities and personality. Now's your chance to go out into the world and use your gifts!

Father, I know You have a plan for me and my life. I'm not sure what it is, but please fill me with Your courage to use the gifts You've given me. Please help me do the good things You've already prepared for me to do!

Rescue

Because he has loved Me, I will bring him out of trouble. I will set him in a safe place on high, because he has known My name. He will call upon Me, and I will answer him. I will be with him in trouble. I will take him out of trouble and honor him.

PSALM 91:14–15

Many fairy tales involve a rescue of some kind. Prince Charming rescued Cinderella. Gretel rescued Hansel. Beauty rescued Beast.

A rescue involves some kind of risk; at some point, the hero or heroine puts everything on the line to attempt the rescue. This is true in literature, in the plots of many movies, and in real life too.

God promises He will rescue those who love Him. He has done it time and time again, and He will continue to do it. If you trust in His name, He will protect you. When you call on Him, He will answer. When you're going through trouble, He will be with you. The Lord will honor and rescue you.

Father, I'm so glad You're my rescuer. I need You!

Trust Fall

You were under the power of the Law. But now you are dead to it because you are joined to another. You are joined to Christ Who was raised from the dead. This is so we may be what God wants us to be.

ROMANS 7:4

If you've ever done a trust fall, you know how difficult it can be to relax to the point of falling backward, hoping that someone will catch you. Sometimes, choosing to follow Jesus can feel like that. Can you trust Him? Will He catch you once you fall?

When you put all your trust in Jesus, He *does* catch you. And He doesn't just catch you; He joins you. You're His. You don't have to worry about Him judging you according to the strict standards of His law. And you won't have to worry about being alone and trying so hard to work in your own strength.

Lord Jesus, it's amazing that You rose from the dead and are alive right now. I trust You completely!

The Sweet Perfume of Jesus

The Good News is like a sweet smell to those who hear it. We are a sweet smell of Christ that reaches up to God. It reaches out to those who are being saved from the punishment of sin and to those who are still lost in sin. It is the smell of death to those who are lost in sin. It is the smell of life to those who are being saved from the punishment of sin.

2 CORINTHIANS 2:14–16

Scents can be a funny thing. Some of your favorite scents in the whole world can smell less than appealing to someone else. One amazing smell to one person might bring up awful memories for someone else.

Your life gives off a scent too. If you love and follow Christ, your life will smell like His aroma. For people who choose not to follow Jesus? His scent is repulsive. But for believers, your life will smell like the sweet perfume of Jesus. You'll smell like life.

Lord Jesus, I want to give off the fragrance of You and Your forever life wherever I go.

Forever

He will take away death for all time. The Lord God will dry tears from all faces. He will take away the shame of His people from all the earth.

ISAIAH 25:8

When you have a bad day (or a bad week!), it's easy to focus on the negative. Wrongs done to you seem larger than life. Little mistakes feel so much bigger. Sometimes all the bad things pile up so that you end up crying over the tiniest matters.

These bad days and frustrations won't last forever. A day is coming when everything awful will be gone. Death will be a thing of the past. You won't cry. In fact, the Lord Himself will wipe away every tear. Insults and mockery? All of that will be gone too.

If it sounds too good to be true, just wait for it. It's coming!

Lord God, it's wonderful to think that tears and insults and death never were part of Your plan. And it's even better to realize that You'll do away with them all. Thank You for promising forever peace!

Your Keeper

The Lord watches over you. The Lord is your safe cover at your right hand. The sun will not hurt you during the day and the moon will not hurt you during the night. The Lord will keep you from all that is sinful. He will watch over your soul. The Lord will watch over your coming and going, now and forever.

PSALM 121:5–8

Even if you tend to be brave, someday you'll need to face your fears with courage.

When you realize you're afraid, it's okay. Acknowledge your fear instead of trying to stuff it deep inside. Then remind yourself that the Lord watches over and protects you during the day and all night long. He will guide you and work in you even in the scariest times. Remember that He's the one who will keep you from harm.

Father, when I'm afraid and it seems like everything is going wrong, help me to remember Your care and to trust in Your protection. Thank You for watching over me!

Much More

God is able to do much more than we ask or think through His power working in us.
Ephesians 3:20

Do you think you have your life figured out? Do you have some idea of what you'd like to do or what you're capable of doing?

Your own plans and ideas might be blown away. You see, right now God is working in you through His own mighty power. He can do things no one else could ever do. And He can accomplish much more in you and through you than you can imagine. You wouldn't even be able to think to ask about some of the amazing things He'll do in your life. Not only is that super exciting, but it also makes Him so very worthy of your praise and worship.

Lord God, I come before You in worship. I praise You! I thank You for doing so much more in my life than I could ever dream.

Shining with Joy

They looked to Him and their faces shined with joy. Their faces will never be ashamed.

PSALM 34:5

On sunny days, the sun is so brilliant that it's natural to squint. Just as the sun is bright and shiny, the more time you spend with God, the more you will reflect His shine. God is infinitely brighter than our solar system's sun. And His brightness naturally rubs off on you the more you get to know Him.

Take some time today to read your Bible. (Wondering what to read? Try one of the Psalms!) Read a few verses and think over what you've observed. Consider how you could apply it to your life. Then pray about what you've read and considered. As you do that day after day, the Lord won't seem so distant. He'll be close to you—and the closer you get, the brighter and shinier you'll be.

Lord, I want to spend more time with You! I want to shine with Your joy.

Gone

Those of us who belong to Christ have nailed our sinful old selves on His cross. Our sinful desires are now dead.

Galatians 5:24

The temptation to sin can seem so strong. In fact, sometimes it feels uncontrollable, like you have to give in.

But if you belong to Christ, you don't have to give in to temptation. In fact, Jesus will give you the strength to stand up against sin. Galatians says that you've nailed your passions and sinful urges to the cross. Those drives and desires are crucified—they're dead. They don't have a hold over you anymore.

Instead of dwelling on the temptations that seem so strong, dwell on the fact that Jesus died so you wouldn't have to be a slave to sin anymore. You're free from the power of sin. Even if it seems like it could entice you, remember that it holds no power over you. Your drive to sin? It's gone!

Lord Jesus, thank You for freedom from sin! Thank You for dying so that my sins wouldn't have a hold on me anymore!

Knowing Your Heart

In the same way, the Holy Spirit helps us where we are weak. We do not know how to pray or what we should pray for, but the Holy Spirit prays to God for us with sounds that cannot be put into words.

ROMANS 8:26

Have you ever felt so confused that you couldn't even put words to the feelings that were rushing through your body? Just as it's not always easy to know what you're thinking or feeling, sometimes you don't know how to pray either.

The amazing news is that the Holy Spirit knows you so well that you don't need to tell Him how you're feeling. He knows. He searches your heart and knows just what you're experiencing. He understands what's grieving you and what's bringing you joy. Be grateful that He knows how to step in and plead on your behalf. He knows you well and loves you very much!

Holy Spirit, I don't praise You enough. I'm so glad You know my heart and do what's best for me. I worship You!

All Things

We know that God makes all things work together for the good of those who love Him and are chosen to be a part of His plan.

Romans 8:28

You might have read Romans 8:28 before: In all things God works for the good of those who love Him. It can be hard to believe though, especially if you're in the middle of an awful time. When you hear heartbreaking news or you're really sick or feel betrayed or disappointed, it seems like nothing good could come from the situation.

Yet God is working good. Even when it doesn't seem possible, God does work all things together for good for those who love Him. If you've been called by Him, according to His purpose, He's working all situations out for your good.

Rest in that truth, even on your worst days. God is for you!

Father, I'm glad I can trust You even on my worst days. Please give me a glimmer of hope and show me something good in my toughest moments. I trust You!

Near to God

But as for me, it is good to be near God. I have made the Lord God my safe place. So I may tell of all the things You have done.

Psalm 73:28

When you have a really good conversation with a close friend, it's natural to sit right next to each other or stand near each other. Deep conversations don't happen when you're farther apart and need to yell at each other to be heard above the noise.

In the same way, if you're going to have a close, meaningful relationship with God, you need to be near Him. If you're far away, you'll never get a chance to really know Him. And if you stay far away long enough, you make it obvious to Him that you don't care.

Build your relationship with God by getting close to Him. When you spend time with Him, He'll become your safe place, your closest friend.

Lord God, I don't want to wait to get close to You—I want to start today.

With You

"The Lord your God is with you, a Powerful One Who wins the battle. He will have much joy over you. With His love He will give you new life. He will have joy over you with loud singing."

ZEPHANIAH 3:17

Did you realize that the Lord your God is with you? He's in the middle of everything in your life. He's not just a quiet bystander who observes everything. He will save you. (He's mighty enough to do that!) He will rejoice over you with gladness. He will give you a new life with His love. He will rejoice over you with loud singing.

The Lord has promised to shower you with His love, cheer you on, and defend you and your cause. He's your number one fan, and He's always with you.

Father, it's amazing that You love me so much and are always cheering me on and wanting what's best for me. Thank You!

Always Listening

I love the Lord, because He hears my voice and my prayers. I will call on Him as long as I live, because He has turned His ear to me.

PSALM 116:1–2

Have you ever tried to get someone else's attention, but they just won't listen to you? Even if they notice you're talking, they don't fully pay attention.

That kind of refusal to listen never happens with the Lord. He hears your voice. He turns His ear to you. He hears your prayers. When you have something to say, He listens. He pays attention. He focuses on what you share with Him.

When you know someone cares so deeply for you that He listens to whatever you have to say, no matter when you say it, you can and should keep talking to Him. Keep sharing what's in your heart and on your mind. He'll listen. And He'll respond out of love.

Lord, it's a relief to know You listen to me! Thank You for caring so much about me that You pay attention to what I have to say.

Live in His Rest

"Come to Me, all of you who work and have heavy loads. I will give you rest. Follow My teachings and learn from Me. I am gentle and do not have pride. You will have rest for your souls. For My way of carrying a load is easy and My load is not heavy."

MATTHEW 11:28–30

When it seems like everything or everyone turns against you, do you start to feel tired? If you think about problems either in your own life or around the world, does it all feel like a heavy load?

Jesus knew this life would weigh you down. But He came to ease your burden. He came to bring you rest.

In His gentle and humble way, Jesus offers a freedom you can't find in anything or anyone else. His freedom is light and easy because it brings your soul rest. Through Jesus you can live, thrive, and be refreshed in His rest.

Lord Jesus, thank You for Your easy way! Thank You for offering me rest. I pray I'll choose to find it in You.

Not Surprising

Dear friends, your faith is going to be tested as if it were going through fire. Do not be surprised at this. Be happy that you are able to share some of the suffering of Christ. When His shining-greatness is shown, you will be filled with much joy.

1 PETER 4:12–13

Just because someone else opposes your belief doesn't make your belief wrong. It just means you have a difference of opinion.

Of all people, Jesus faced opposition. He knew He was the Son of God, and He wasn't afraid to admit it—even when it cost Him His life. Just as Jesus suffered when He stood up for truth, you can expect to suffer for the sake of Him and His truth too.

When you do suffer, you can be glad—it means you're like Jesus! You're sharing His suffering. While that sounds pretty awful to experience, the amazing news is that all of your suffering will end in joy.

Lord Jesus, I believe in You! I know You're true. Please prepare me to suffer for You and Your truth if necessary.

Every Need!

My God will give you everything you need
because of His great riches in Christ Jesus.
PHILIPPIANS 4:19

When you belong to the Lord, He takes care of you in a sweet, generous way.

In His love and care for you, He supplies every need of yours. You may not even need to ask Him ahead of time because He knows what you need even before you ask. He has promised to meet every single one of your needs according to His riches in glory. He'll pour them out for you so you're filled to overflowing.

If you stop to think about that, it's pretty amazing. There's no way to imagine the riches that are found in Christ's glory, yet God is ready to heap them on and shower you with them. What a generous, caring, giving heavenly Father!

Father, not only do You know my needs, but You also meet them by generously pouring out Your gifts on me. Thank You for sharing with me!

Pick a Side

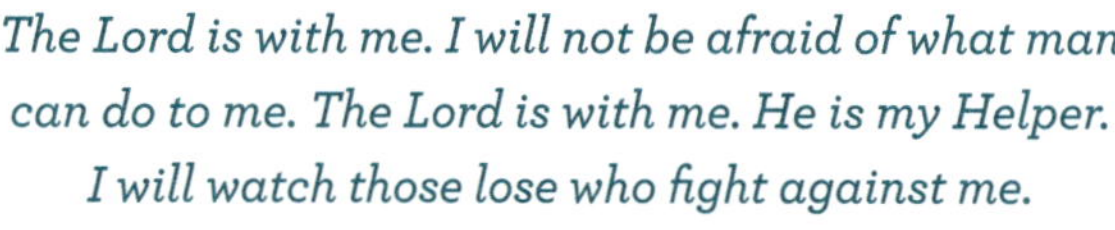

The Lord is with me. I will not be afraid of what man can do to me. The Lord is with me. He is my Helper. I will watch those lose who fight against me.

Psalm 118:6–7

Have you ever felt pressure to pick a side? Once you decide, it automatically eliminates the other side. You've made your choice.

When asked about you, the Lord chose you to be on His side. He made His decision. He picked *you*. Now that you're on His side, He's ready and willing to help you. If and when people fight you, know that God is on your side. If your opponents try to say or do hurtful things to you, know that God is with you. You don't have to fear. You don't have to worry and wonder what might happen. Without a doubt, the Lord is your defender.

Lord, thank You for picking me to be on Your side! It's such a comfort and relief to know You're with me!

Are You Connected?

"No branch can give fruit by itself. It has to get life from the vine. You are able to give fruit only when you have life from Me. I am the Vine and you are the branches. Get your life from Me. Then I will live in you and you will give much fruit. You can do nothing without Me."

JOHN 15:4–5

After a windstorm, try picking up branches that have fallen off trees. You can watch those branches for a long time and nothing will change—well, unless the leaves wither and fall off.

Just like a branch can't grow or thrive or bear fruit if it's not connected to an actual living tree, you can't thrive or bear fruit for the Lord if you're not connected to Him. As much as you may hope to do things on your own, it just won't happen. You can't bear fruit unless you remain in Him. Be thankful that through Christ you will bear much fruit.

Jesus, I want to remain in You! Please help me do much for You!

Listen to His Words

"So My Word which goes from My mouth will not return to Me empty. It will do what I want it to do, and will carry out My plan well."

ISAIAH 55:11

Did you know that God's Word is living and active? According to Hebrews 4:12 it is, and it also judges the thoughts and attitudes of the heart. That can't be said of any other piece of literature!

Just as amazingly, God's Word doesn't return empty. When you hear the Bible, the Lord will use it to achieve a certain purpose. His Word will be used to accomplish His plan.

The Bible isn't a randomly chosen group of stories. It's truth, and God uses it to teach you, correct you, train you, and equip you for life. The more you listen to it, read it, and obey it, the more deeply it will change you!

Father, thank You so much for Your Word! Please use it in my life to accomplish Your purposes.

Perfect Power

He answered me, "I am all you need. I give you My loving-favor. My power works best in weak people." I am happy to be weak and have troubles so I can have Christ's power in me.

2 CORINTHIANS 12:9

Some days you simply don't have strength to do what you need to do. Maybe you don't understand a project that's due. Maybe you've been asked to help out in some way but you have little interest. Or maybe you're really excited about a certain event but are overwhelmed and exhausted with all the preparation.

Whatever the situation, know this: Jesus' power is made perfect in your weakness. When you're weak, He is strong. And when you acknowledge you can't do something on your own and you ask Him for help, He will help—every single time. The power of Christ will rest on you when you're weak. That's way more power than you could ever produce on your own!

Lord Jesus, thank You for giving me strength! Please help me remember that when I am weak, You are strong.

He Knew

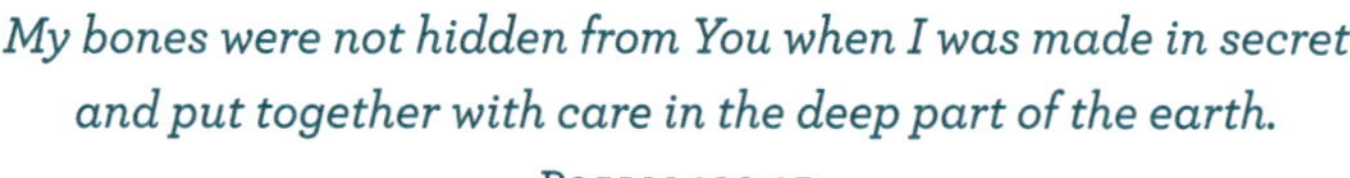

My bones were not hidden from You when I was made in secret and put together with care in the deep part of the earth.

Psalm 139:15

Long before your mother even knew you existed, God knew. He began making you in secret with a master plan. He knew just what you needed to be you. No one else in the world has ever looked or sounded or thought like you, and no one ever will. No one has ever had your unique set of gifts and talents, and no one ever will. You're uniquely you, and God created you to be just the way you are!

Just as the Lord knew His plans for you even before you were born, He certainly knows you now! Not a moment goes by when He isn't thinking of you or paying attention to what you're thinking, saying, or doing. From your best days to your worst days, the Lord has a wonderful plan for you.

Father, You know me like no one else! Thank You for knowing exactly who I am and choosing to love me anyway.

Living in Light

At one time you lived in darkness.
Now you are living in the light that
comes from the Lord. Live as children
who have the light of the Lord in them.
EPHESIANS 5:8

Throughout life, you're either one thing or another. You're either awake or asleep. You're either in school or out of school. You're either in the darkness or in the light.

When it comes to knowing Jesus, there's no way to walk with or live in Him unless He is in you. No Jesus? No life and no light from the Lord. But if you do know Jesus, you do have life and light in Him.

If Jesus really is in you, it's time to start obeying what He asks of you out of love. You'll choose to do what He has asked you to do, even when you need to put your own choices aside. If Jesus really is in you, it's time to let His light shine in your life!

Lord Jesus, I love You and want to live in Your light!

Mindfulness

When I look up and think about Your heavens, the work of Your fingers, the moon and the stars, which You have set in their place, what is man, that You think of him, the son of man that You care for him?

PSALM 8:3–4

Have you taken time to look up at the night sky? Those tiny stars are trillions of miles away, yet you can see them sparkle brightly from where they are set in just the place the Lord designed.

Creation holds so many secrets we'll never discover, yet God knows exactly how He created everything. He also knows why He created everything in certain ways.

When you consider how detailed everything is, from the microscopic cells in your body to the beautiful petals of a flower, it's astounding to think that God created humans in His image. And He sent His only Son to this world as a human to rescue us. That's a mindful God who loves you completely!

Father, thank You for caring for me! Your creation is beautiful. Thank You for choosing to love human beings the way You do!

Transformer

But whenever a man turns to the Lord, the covering is taken away. . . . All of us, with no covering on our faces, show the shining-greatness of the Lord as in a mirror. All the time we are being changed to look like Him, with more and more of His shining-greatness. This change is from the Lord Who is the Spirit.

2 CORINTHIANS 3:16, 18

If you've ever watched makeover shows, you know that whether it's a home or someone's style that's getting updated, the big reveal is usually pretty drastic! It's fun to see proof of "before" and "after" a transformation.

If you've asked Jesus to become Lord of your life, you've experienced your own makeover. Your life was one way before you came to know Jesus. But once you turned to Him, you experienced freedom in your soul. Suddenly you were able to reflect His glory. That makeover changed your heart and your soul.

Father, being transformed by You is such a gift. Thank You for making me over through faith in Jesus!

More Than Works

God, the One Who saves, showed how kind He was and how He loved us by saving us from the punishment of sin. It was not because we worked to be right with God. It was because of His loving-kindness that He washed our sins away.

TITUS 3:4–5

It can be easy to think you deserve something. If you treat people with kindness, you think you deserve kindness in return. When you study hard for a test, you think you deserve a good grade. If you do good things, you think you deserve favor.

But that's not the way God looks at things. Even if you try hard to please Him through good works, it doesn't matter. Instead of checking on how much good you've done, the Lord looks at your heart and what you believe. Do you trust in His Son? If so, He saves you from punishment. You can't save yourself, but He can save you.

Lord Jesus, thank You for Your goodness and love! Thank You for saving me according to Your own mercy!

Such a Time as This

"For if you keep quiet at this time, help will come to the Jews from another place. But you and your father's house will be destroyed. Who knows if you have not become queen for such a time as this?"

ESTHER 4:14

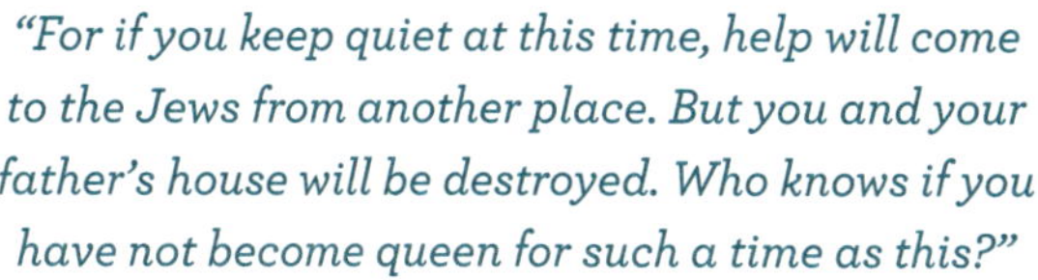

God knew that out of all moments throughout time, this would be your moment to shine. He planned for you to live right here and right now. He has a plan for you to live and think and speak in this current world.

Today's world needs to hear your voice. And as you share the love of Christ, you can start making a difference in the people around you. You'll affect your very own corner of the world.

Just as Queen Esther was encouraged by her cousin Mordecai, his wise words apply to you too: "Who knows if you have not [come]. . .for such a time as this?"

Father, please help me bravely stand up for Your truth today. Thank You for planning my life to happen during this moment in history.

All You Need

God can give you all you need. He will give you more than enough. You will have everything you need for yourselves. And you will have enough left over to give when there is a need.

2 Corinthians 9:8

Have you stopped to think about the way God gives you absolutely everything you need? Everything you think you might earn or deserve or that comes as a gift from someone else actually is provided by your heavenly Father. He uses different ways to provide, but He still makes sure you're taken care of very well.

Once you thank Him for providing everything for you, make sure you share your wealth! Use what you need, but when you have extra—whether it's food or clothing or other possessions—copy the Lord's generosity and share your good gifts with someone else. When you do, your life and giving will look more and more like the Lord's.

Father, it's such a relief to know You'll always give me everything I need so that I have plenty left over to share with others. Thanks! You take such good care of me!

Ready to Start?

Now that we have been made right with God by putting our trust in Him, we have peace with Him. It is because of what our Lord Jesus Christ did for us. By putting our trust in God, He has given us His loving-favor and has received us.

ROMANS 5:1–2

When you play board games like Candy Land, each game begins with the first space. Once you're ready to play, you place your piece on the space marked "Start," then move on by drawing cards.

In much the same way, faith in Christ is the start of your Christian life. Faith is the starting space you need before you can continue. When you believe through faith, you're ready to start the rest of your journey of a life lived in peace with God. Your new life includes privilege with God that you don't deserve. And you can joyfully and confidently wait for the big finish: living in the presence of the living God in all His glory.

Father, I want to start my life with You, and through Jesus, I want to be at peace with You. I trust in Him!

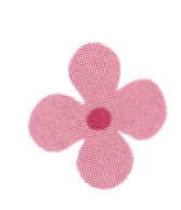

Sheepish

Come, let us bow down in worship. Let us get down on our knees before the Lord Who made us. For He is our God. And we are the people of His field, and the sheep of His hand.

Psalm 95:6–7

Sheep follow their shepherd anywhere and everywhere. They trust their shepherd to feed them and lead them. In fact, they only respond to their shepherd's call.

Just as sheep know and listen to their shepherd, you can choose to know and obey the Lord. Jesus is the good shepherd—so good that He laid down His life for His sheep. His followers are like His sheep. As a loving leader and shepherd, He is worthy of all your praise. He is your Maker. He is your God. He is your shepherd.

Lord Jesus, I worship You! Thank You for leading me so well. And thank You for giving Your life so I might live forever. Please help me stick near You like a sheep since You are the good shepherd.

Live Worthy

I ask you from my heart to live and work the way the Lord expected you to live and work. Live and work without pride. Be gentle and kind. Do not be hard on others. Let love keep you from doing that. Work hard to live together as one by the help of the Holy Spirit. Then there will be peace.

EPHESIANS 4:1–3

Because God chose you to belong to Him, it's only right that you live in a way that reflects His gift. If you're wondering what that looks like, the Bible gives details in Ephesians 4: Set aside your pride. Be gentle and kind. Out of love and for the sake of peace, accept others and try to live as one.

This kind of life definitely is different than the way most people live. But instead of caving in and living like everyone else, choose to live the way God asks out of your thankfulness and love for Him.

Lord Jesus, it's not always easy to live the way You'd like me to live. I want to live full of Your love, patience, and kindness!

Loved and Forgiven

For His loving-kindness for those who fear Him is as great as the heavens are high above the earth. He has taken our sins from us as far as the east is from the west.

PSALM 103:11–12

When you belong to Christ, God looks at you differently. Not only does He love you and shower you with His favor, but He also pours out His forgiveness on you. In fact, He loves you so much that the Bible describes the greatness as being as high as the heavens are above the earth.

And His forgiveness? Through Jesus, God has He has removed your sins as far as the east is from the west. Just take one step outside and look to the east. Then turn around and look to the west. Both directions seem to run in separate directions forever, right? That's how huge God's forgiveness is!

Lord, I can't understand the scope of Your love or Your forgiveness. But I'm so grateful for both of them! Thank You for loving me more than I ever can imagine and for forgiving me so much more than I deserve.

His Mission

"For God did not send His Son into the world to say it is guilty. He sent His Son so the world might be saved from the punishment of sin by Him. Whoever puts his trust in His Son is not guilty. Whoever does not put his trust in Him is guilty already. It is because he does not put his trust in the name of the only Son of God."

JOHN 3:17–18

Have you ever thought about why God the Father would send His only Son into the world? Jesus could have stayed in heaven forever to experience the honor, praise, and worship He deserves. But He humbled Himself and came to this earth in a life of humility instead of riches or royalty.

Jesus was sent on this rescue mission for one reason: to save those who would trust Him. He wasn't sent to judge the world.

Once you believe in the name of the only Son of God, you are rescued from judgment and guilt. You are saved and set free through your trust in Him.

Jesus, thank You for being so willing to rescue those who trust You!

Special Treatment

The Lord is near to all who call on Him, to all who call on Him in truth. He will fill the desire of those who fear Him. He will also hear their cry and will save them. The Lord takes care of all who love Him. But He will destroy all the sinful.

Psalm 145:18–20

When you belong to the Lord, you get special treatment. (Who doesn't like that?!) Naturally you call on Him, fear Him with great respect, and love Him with all your heart. Because of this, the Lord is close to you. He'll hear your cries for help and rescue you. He'll grant your desires and protect you.

Just as you're more willing to listen and respond to someone you know and love very well, the Lord does the same with you. He responds to you with much love and concern because you're His.

Lord God, I do love You! And I come to You today with respect because You are Lord of all. Thank You for taking such special care of me.

Free to Serve

Obey as men who are free but do not use this to cover up sin. Live as servants owned by God at all times.

1 PETER 2:16

Through Jesus, you're not a slave to sin anymore. Jesus has set you free, and He doesn't want you to take advantage of God's forgiveness by continuing to sin. Instead, you can choose to do what's right and serve the Lord. This service overflows out of your love for Him. Are you truly grateful for all He has done for you? Then show it by the way you serve Him!

Love looks like joyfully serving those you love. You may not always enjoy doing certain things, but you can do those tasks in love. For example, your parents probably didn't always love changing your dirty diapers when you were a baby, but they did it out of their intense love for you. Similarly, you can choose to serve God out of love, no matter what.

Father, I love You! I'm thankful You saved me from the slavery of sin. I want to serve You out of my love for You!

Go Right In

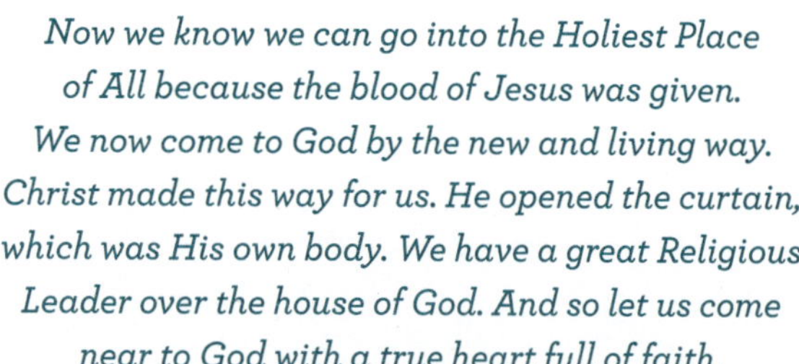

Now we know we can go into the Holiest Place of All because the blood of Jesus was given. We now come to God by the new and living way. Christ made this way for us. He opened the curtain, which was His own body. We have a great Religious Leader over the house of God. And so let us come near to God with a true heart full of faith.

HEBREWS 10:19–22

In the Old Testament, Israelite priests could enter the Holy Place after meeting many strict rules and following many religious duties.

Things changed with Jesus. When He died, the curtain between the Holy Place and Most Holy Place was torn in two. He was the sacrifice that took away our sins. He now sits as the great High Priest who rules over God's house and is the one who steps in on your behalf.

Today, because of Jesus, you can go right into God's presence. He lives and is able to save you.

Lord Jesus, I want to come near You with a true heart full of faith!

Night and Day

Because we are men of the day, let us keep our minds awake. Let us cover our chests with faith and love. Let us cover our heads with the hope of being saved.

1 THESSALONIANS 5:8

When you think about day and night, you notice an obvious difference between the two: light. During the day, things are light because of the sun. But once the sun sets, everything is dark.

Just like the obvious difference between day and night, there's a noticeable contrast between those who believe in Christ and those who don't. Believers live in light because the Light of the world is a part of them and clearly lights the way. But those who don't believe live in darkness. They stumble around, just like being stuck outside in the middle of the night without a flashlight.

If you have the light of Christ, live like it! You don't have to fear the darkness anymore!

Jesus, thank You for shining Your light into my heart. I want to trust You completely and show the world that I'm living in Your light.

Together!

See, how good and how pleasing it is for brothers to live together as one!

Psalm 133:1

If you belong to Christ, it's important to remember you're not the only one who does. In fact, you can't even count all your sisters and brothers in Christ! Believers from all around the world share a common belief with you: Jesus is alive and He is Lord of all.

Since you're just one member of God's huge family, it's important to remember that you're part of a family. As much as it's possible, don't get hung up on your differences. Instead, remember what unifies you: Christ! Stay united in His love, and try to encourage and support each other because of that unity.

Because you'll get to spend eternity together, now's a perfect time to practice some family unity!

Father God, it's exciting to think that I'm a part of Your family along with people from every nation. Please help me to be a good sister in Christ by seeking ways to be united with other believers.

Measuring Up

All of us are to be as one in the faith and in knowing the Son of God. We are to be full-grown Christians standing as high and complete as Christ is Himself.

EPHESIANS 4:13

Have you ever been compared to someone else? Usually it doesn't feel so great to wonder if you're measuring up to someone else. In fact, comparison can make you feel insecure or uncertain.

Yet Christ has set a standard. (Spoiler alert: It's impossible to meet that standard on your own!) Anyone who believes in Him is on a lifelong adventure of measuring up to His standard through the power of the Holy Spirit within. You just keep growing more and more like Jesus.

As you grow, God will also use other believers in your life who will do His work and build you up. Welcome that help, because it will help you measure up to Christ's standard!

Lord, it's scary to think about measuring up to Christ's standard, but I'm glad I don't have to figure it out on my own. Thank You for sending Your Holy Spirit and other believers into my life to help me!

Kindness Is Cool

"Love those who hate you. Do good to them. Let them use your things and do not expect something back. Your reward will be much. You will be the children of the Most High. He is kind to those who are not thankful and to those who are full of sin."

Luke 6:35

If someone is mean to you, a natural response is to repay that cruelty. But instead of looking for ways to get payback, do what God asks you to do, which is something completely different: Love instead of hate. Be kind instead of cruel. Do good instead of evil. Be compassionate instead of nasty.

Loving your enemies is hard. It seems to go against everything that feels natural. But you're not asked to do what's natural. Just as God is kind to truly awful people, He'll give you power to do the same. When it feels hard, ask God to help. Then do good, even to your enemies.

Father, Your ability to love and be kind and compassionate to the wicked is absolutely amazing. I want to learn from You! Please help me!

A Generous Giver

From Him Who has so much we have all received loving-favor, one loving-favor after another.

JOHN 1:16

Who is the most generous person you know? How much and how often does that person give to others? How does their generosity make you feel—especially if you're on the receiving end?

Take that most generous person and multiply their generosity by about a billion. Even then you won't come close to getting a good picture of the Lord's abundance and generosity.

God gives and gives and gives. It's in His character to pour out His blessings on everyone—especially those who belong to Him. Just as a loving earthly father typically gives his child good gifts, God does even more. And He doesn't just wait until your birthday or holidays to give you something—He gives and gives every day.

When you experience the Lord's gifts and blessings, thank Him! Be grateful for the gifts you recognize right away, and thank Him when you realize what good gifts His unexpected blessings are.

Thank You, Father! You've filled my life with such good gifts.

Forgiveness

Will You be angry with us forever? Will You spread out Your anger to families of all times? Will You not bring us back to life again so that Your people may be happy in You?

Psalm 85:5–6

When you've wronged someone, it's easy to feel embarrassed and ashamed. You wish you could have a redo, where you go back and make sure things happen differently. Sometimes, in the middle of all your awkwardness and guilt, the person you've wronged offers forgiveness. They don't hold a grudge against you, and it's as if nothing ever happened.

Whether you realize it or not, you end up wronging God every day. But when you confess your sins and ask Him for forgiveness, He willingly forgives. And once God forgives you, He won't hold a grudge.

As awkward as it might feel, come to God and admit your sins. Ask for His forgiveness. Then soak in His great love.

Lord, I confess that I've sinned against You. Please forgive me!

A Different Kind of Life

Last of all, you must share the same thoughts and the same feelings. Love each other with a kind heart and with a mind that has no pride.

1 PETER 3:8

When you choose to follow God, you choose to live differently than those around you. When you realize that God is God and you're not, your pride will start to disappear and you'll have a better, humbler picture of yourself.

You'll start to look at other people differently too. Instead of judging them, you'll try to see things from other people's points of view and understand what they're facing. Through the Holy Spirit's power, you'll be able to love people really well. You won't just say that you're a loving person—you'll actually love in a kind, caring way that only comes from God.

Father God, I want to live differently than so many people in this world who say one thing and do another thing. I want to love well, just like You do. Through Your Holy Spirit, please help me to be more like You!

In Times of Trouble

God is our safe place and our strength.
He is always our help when we are in trouble.
Psalm 46:1

It's easy to stress out when you feel bullied or trapped, either by unfair situations or people with cruel intentions. When you don't know what to do, tell everything to the Lord. Tell Him your worries. Talk to Him about your fears and concerns and doubts. Go ahead and keep telling Him all that you're thinking, including all the "what-ifs" that keep you up at night.

As you tell God everything, ask for His help. Since He's Lord of all creation, He has much more power than you can begin to imagine. As your safe place, He's able and willing to protect you from danger and hardship. When you run to Him, He's always ready to help you in times of trouble. And He's always ready to be your strength, even when it feels like you don't have any.

Father, I need Your help! And I need Your strength and protection to make it through my troubles today.

No Matter Who

"We believe it is by the loving-favor of the Lord Jesus that we are saved. They are saved from the punishment of sin the same way."

ACTS 15:11

This world is filled with all kinds of people who believe all kinds of different things. All of those differences can be celebrated. Yet no matter who a person is, there's only one way to be saved: by the grace of Jesus.

It doesn't matter what a person does—whether they focus on doing good or focus on pleasing themselves—not a single person deserves or earns the grace of Jesus.

This means the playing field is leveled. You don't have an advantage over anyone else. No matter who you're related to, where you come from, or how you've been raised, you have just as much need for Jesus as anyone else you see. Through faith, it's Jesus' grace that saves you. No matter who you are, you need Jesus.

Lord Jesus, I need You! I trust You and believe You alone can save me!

The Perfect Person for You

Your eyes saw me before I was put together. And all the days of my life were written in Your book before any of them came to be.

Psalm 139:16

Have you ever wished someone would know you—all of you, from your strengths to your weaknesses—and still accept and love you completely?

What if the perfect person for you isn't someone you'll ever meet in the flesh? What if that perfect person for you has known you for your entire existence?

Living, breathing, real people can't meet all of your needs. As much as you hope for a soul mate, no one person will ever fulfill you. The more people you get to know, the more you'll realize this. Instead of being disappointed time and time again, turn to the limitless one. He created you. He has planned all the days of your life. He knows you completely and loves you completely.

My Lord and my God, I praise You! It's amazing that You know me completely and absolutely love me.

No Penalty

Anyone can be made right with God by the free gift of His loving-favor. It is Jesus Christ Who bought them with His blood and made them free from their sins.

ROMANS 3:24

Whether you're playing sports or concentrating on school rules or obeying the law, you don't want to get a penalty. Getting punished and facing consequences for breaking a law or rule is never enjoyable. Disobedience always results in consequences, no matter the situation.

When you sin, you deserve a penalty. God knows that the penalty for sinning is harsh: It's forever separation from Him.

Since He created you and loves you, He offers you a way out of the punishment and penalty. When you believe in Jesus, God makes you right in His sight. Jesus took care of your penalty. Your punishment is paid for.

God has given you this huge, undeserved gift. But like any gift, it's not yours until you receive it and open it up. What are you waiting for?

Father, I'm relieved that because of Jesus, I don't have to worry about the penalty for my sins.

Fear Factor

How great is Your loving-kindness! You have stored it up for those who fear You. You show it to those who trust in You in front of the sons of men.

Psalm 31:19

We live in a world where we're taught to avoid fear. So what in the world does the Bible mean when it says to fear the Lord? Fearing the Lord doesn't involve danger. Rather, it means you respect the God of the universe with awe and reverence for who He is.

God stores up goodness for those who fear Him and then lavishes His goodness on them. Plus, according to Proverbs, the fear of the Lord is a fountain of life that leads to rest and satisfaction (Proverbs 14:27). It's also the beginning of wisdom (Proverbs 9:10).

When you honor and respect God for who He is, He really will bless you!

Father, You are truly great. I'm in awe that You're Lord of all and still regard me. I have so much respect for You!

What's Amazing about Grace?

I am thankful to God all the time for you.
I am thankful for the loving-favor God has given
to you because you belong to Christ Jesus.
1 CORINTHIANS 1:4

Grace is an undeserved gift of loving favor. In other words, you don't do anything to make yourself worthy to receive God's favor. God, being the giver of all good gifts, decided to go all out and surprise you with an amazing gift: He blesses you instead of cursing you.

You're undeserving of His blessing—everyone is!—yet the Lord chose to give it to you anyway because He's full of love and kindness. The miracle of grace is that God chose to make a way for you to enter a relationship with Him, and that way is through Jesus. When you say yes to Christ, you say yes to accepting God's good gift of grace. You choose to unwrap that gift and make it your own.

My Lord, thank You! Thank You for Your amazing gift of grace. Thank You for offering it to me through Jesus.

Get Your Head in the Game

*Get your minds ready for good use. Keep awake.
Set your hope now and forever on the loving-favor to
be given you when Jesus Christ comes again.*

1 PETER 1:13

God's gift of grace to you—blessing instead of cursing—is something you can count on and celebrate. But while you can experience parts of His fantastic favor right now, you won't get to fully understand it until Jesus returns.

In the meantime, you have a life to live. And your life will include plenty of choices. How can you live while you're in the middle of waiting? Peter, one of Jesus' closest friends, shared a really practical way: Get your mind ready for action!

A lot of your everyday decisions need self-control. That means you won't always be able to do or say what you really feel. As you choose how to live for Christ, remember you're His messenger in this world. Act like one!

Lord Jesus, it's hard to wait for You! Help me as I try to be Your example in this world.

Light in Darkness

"I came to the world to be a Light. Anyone who puts his trust in Me will not be in darkness."

JOHN 12:46

Think about a time when you've been in total darkness. It's easy to fumble and stumble around when you can't tell what your surroundings are like.

Now think about what your dark experience would be like if you have a flashlight. Totally different, right? You wouldn't have to worry about what might be around you. You'd know how to make your way safely to your destination, and you wouldn't have to fear the unknowns that might be lurking in the dark.

Without Jesus, this world is a dark, dark place. Without Him, everything seems confusing and scary. But if you have the light of Jesus, you don't have to stay in the darkness anymore! You can know the right way to go. Keep your eyes focused on His light. Instead of wandering back into the darkness, stay close to Him, and He'll safely guide you through this life!

Lord Jesus, I'm so thankful You guide me with Your light!

Rooted in Love

I pray that you will be able to understand how wide and how long and how high and how deep His love is. I pray that you will know the love of Christ. His love goes beyond anything we can understand.

EPHESIANS 3:18–19

If you examine a big, healthy tree, you might notice leaves and branches. But keep looking, and it's impossible to miss the incredible root system. Roots keep a tree well grounded even when fierce wind gusts and devastating storms pass, and they keep trees watered and nourished.

Just like a tree, you need good roots too, or else the storms of life will topple you. But what kind of roots will both nourish and ground you?

The love of Christ roots and grounds you in an amazing way. As you experience His love, you'll have an accurate picture of how wide and long and high and deep His love really is.

Lord Jesus, Your love is amazing. It's beyond wonderful to be loved by You!

Playing Favorites

Since God is for us, who can be against us? God did not keep His own Son for Himself but gave Him for us all. Then with His Son, will He not give us all things? Who can say anything against the people God has chosen? It is God Who says they are right with Himself.

ROMANS 8:31–33

What's one of your absolute favorite things in the whole world? In your eyes, your favorite thing is amazing. You can't find many (if any) faults in it, and you could definitely describe yourself as being "for" that favorite thing—never, ever against it.

Did you know that God has His own list of favorites too? And did you know that you're on that list? Just like you're for your favorite things, God is for you. He has chosen you for His own. No one and nothing can condemn you. He gave the very best—His one and only Son!—just for you. He really loves you that much!

Father, I'm not sure why You chose me to be one of Your favorites, but I'm so glad You did!

Committed and Strengthened

"For the eyes of the Lord move over all the earth so that He may give strength to those whose whole heart is given to Him."
2 CHRONICLES 16:9

All throughout the Bible, we're reminded of how God sees us and knows us. He knows our hearts and He knows our minds. Our thoughts and intentions aren't hidden from Him.

Because God knows all people, He knows exactly who loves Him. And He knows exactly who is committed to Him. He knows when someone only says that they love or believe Him, and He knows when people actually do love Him or believe Him.

When God knows your heart is fully given over to Him, He will help you. He'll support you. He'll strengthen you.

O Lord, You know all. You see my heart, and You know every detail about me. I pray You'll find me fully committed to You!

Chosen and Called

But God chose me before I was born.
By His loving-favor He called me to work for Him.
GALATIANS 1:15

In this world, it's easy to believe you need to earn favor. If you could just work hard enough or do the right thing, you could get what you want. You might even be worth more in someone else's eyes.

God doesn't think or act like that. It doesn't matter how hard you work. You don't have to know the "right" people, and you don't have to do the "right" thing. God chose you when you had absolutely nothing to offer. He chose you long before you were born and before you could choose Him.

By His loving-favor, He called you to be His. What you can choose to do is thank and praise Him for His great gift!

Father! It's amazing to know You chose and called me to be Yours even before I was born. I am humbled by and thankful for Your decision and Your favor.

More like Him

Do not act like the sinful people of the world. Let God change your life. First of all, let Him give you a new mind. Then you will know what God wants you to do. And the things you do will be good and pleasing and perfect.

ROMANS 12:2

With one bite of the forbidden fruit in the Garden of Eden, people who once glorified God turned against Him. Because of this, it should come as no surprise that today most people in the world are centered on themselves instead of the Lord.

When you decide to follow the Lord, you want to become more like Him and less like the world. Learn from Him, both in prayer and by reading the Bible. As you do, you'll become less and less like the world and more and more like Him.

Lord, please give me a new mind and change the way I think so I'm not copying what the world says or does.

A Helper

"The Helper is the Holy Spirit. The Father will send Him in My place. He will teach you everything and help you remember everything I have told you."

JOHN 14:26

Trying to figure out how to live like God's daughter can feel confusing and overwhelming, especially when the world tries so hard to influence your thoughts and decisions. But God's way is so very different from the world's.

Fortunately, God doesn't make you try to figure out His way on your own. He has given you the Bible for you to read, study, and understand. And He has given you an amazing gift: His Holy Spirit. Once you ask Jesus to be Lord of your life, the Holy Spirit comes to help you. He teaches you the truth. He guides you in the way you should go. He pricks your conscience when you sin. He is God living in you.

Lord, I don't understand how the Holy Spirit can live in me, but I'm grateful You've sent Him to help me! Please help me fully appreciate what a good gift He is.

Your Instruction Manual

All the Holy Writings are God-given and are made alive by Him. Man is helped when he is taught God's Word. It shows what is wrong. It changes the way of a man's life. It shows him how to be right with God. It gives the man who belongs to God everything he needs to work well for Him.

2 TIMOTHY 3:16–17

Have you ever started a big project without any instructions? Unless you were expecting a completely creative result, how did everything turn out?

Instruction manuals tell you the right order and right way to proceed. Not only do you save time by following instructions, but when you don't have to guess at what to do, you also have a lot less frustration.

Just as directions make tasks easier, the Bible is a fantastic instruction manual. Scripture is helpful for all sorts of things, from teaching you to correcting you. All you need to do is read it—and follow the instructions!

Father, thank You for Your Word! Please help me follow Your directions.

Save Me!

If you say with your mouth that Jesus is Lord,
and believe in your heart that God raised Him from the
dead, you will be saved from the punishment of sin.

ROMANS 10:9

You might have heard that "Jesus saves." But from what does He save you? And how does He save you?

Everyone sins. Those sins keep you from a relationship with God; because of them you deserve punishment. But God didn't want you to be separated from Him or punished. Out of His mercy, He sent Jesus to be punished on your behalf.

The thing is, you have to know and trust in what Jesus did for you. When you do that, you can accept the gift—the fact that He traded His life for yours. You can believe in your heart that He really, truly is Lord. When you believe, you're made right with God. And when you say what you believe, you'll be saved. What will you choose?

Lord Jesus, I believe You are my Lord!
And I believe that God raised You from the dead
and You are alive today. Please save me!

Can You Taste It?

O taste and see that the Lord is good.
How happy is the man who trusts in Him!

PSALM 34:8

What's your favorite flavor? Some people prefer salty foods; others prefer sweet. You might be partial to something sour, or bitter foods might even tempt your taste buds.

Whatever flavor you like to savor, the Lord created them all—and He created an enormous variety of foods for you to enjoy. The next time you eat, slow down and notice the flavors in each bite. What does everything taste like? What tastes really good to you?

As you enjoy each flavorful bite, praise your heavenly Father for giving you vivid senses like taste. Then thank Him for filling your days with food that tastes so unique. He has given a huge variety of flavors, and He has given you a tongue to taste them all. Thank Him and praise Him for those good gifts!

Father God, thank You for food! It's a good gift! When I taste it and like the flavors, I know that You are a good, good God.

It's Your Choice!

"The one who loves Me is the one who has My teaching and obeys it. My Father will love whoever loves Me. I will love him and will show Myself to him."

JOHN 14:21

If you like being free to do what you want to do, obeying someone else can feel like it's holding you back. But if the person you're obeying is trustworthy and ultimately has your best interests in mind, their commands are worth obeying.

You don't have to obey Jesus' commands, but that decision holds consequences. If you do choose to accept and obey His commands, you're showing God your love and devotion.

Once you show your love through obedience, God the Father will show His love to you. God the Son will show His love to you. And, with much love, God the Spirit will come to live in you. God's love and favor hinge on your choice of obedience. What do you choose?

Lord Jesus, obeying You shows my love and acceptance of You. I give my life to You today and will follow Your ways by the help of Your Holy Spirit in me.

Your Citizenship

But we are citizens of heaven. Christ, the One Who saves from the punishment of sin, will be coming down from heaven again. We are waiting for Him to return.

PHILIPPIANS 3:20

When you're a citizen of a place, you know you belong. As a citizen, you're offered protection, privilege, and responsibility.

When you commit your life to Jesus Christ as the Lord of your life, you gain citizenship in heaven. Until you fully realize your citizenship there by actually experiencing your heavenly home, you must wait to meet your Savior face to face.

But as you wait, don't forget that this earth isn't your forever home. You're not a permanent resident or citizen here. Nevertheless, you can make the most of your time by serving God in this temporary residence while waiting for and wondering about your forever, heavenly home!

Lord Jesus, I'm waiting for You! I can't imagine what my heavenly home will be like, but I know You will be there! Thanks for the protection and privilege that come with being a citizen of heaven!

Made Right

Christ never sinned but God put our sin on Him. Then we are made right with God because of what Christ has done for us.

2 CORINTHIANS 5:21

Have you ever had to take someone else's punishment? Maybe you were wrongly accused, and whoever actually misbehaved got away without any consequences. Suffering punishment that is not rightfully yours is not enjoyable, is it?

Most people wouldn't jump at the chance to receive someone else's punishment. In fact, it's typical to try to get out of punishment and consequences completely, even if you absolutely deserve them.

Jesus is different. He came to earth on a rescue mission—specifically to rescue you from the punishment of your sin. That's pretty sacrificial, loving, and kind! As a result of His rescue, you're made right with God through Christ.

Without Jesus, the punishment would be yours and you would be considered at odds with God. But with Jesus and His willingness to take your punishment for sins, you're made right with God!

Lord Jesus, thank You for coming to rescue me and taking my punishment so I could be made right with God.

How Rich?

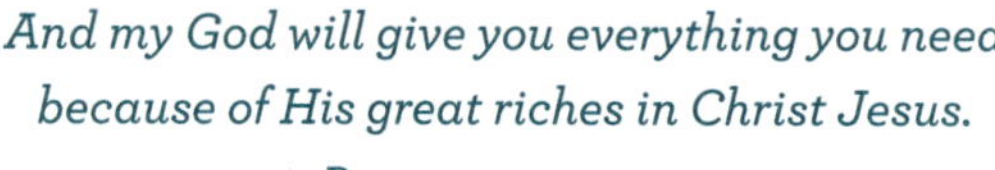

And my God will give you everything you need because of His great riches in Christ Jesus.

PHILIPPIANS 4:19

If you like making plans, you may feel frustrated when the future seems unclear. What will happen? What should you do? You might want to mentally map out the next phase of your life: Who will your friends be? What should you do with your life? When you're old enough to choose, where should you live?

These big questions are worth pondering. They're worth praying about too. Yet as much as you ponder and pray, you don't have to worry about those questions—or their answers. No matter how sketchy the future may seem, God will give you everything you need. Everything!

God won't just supply everything with a bare minimum. He'll supply your needs according to His riches in glory. You can trust Him and rest when you're wondering about your future, for He'll give you everything you need and more!

Father, You are so great! Thank You for providing for every single one of my needs so I don't have to worry.

Always Learning

"And now, my brothers, I give you over to God and to the word of His love. It is able to make you strong and to give you what you are to have, along with all those who are set apart for God."

ACTS 20:32

Throughout your life, you'll meet many teachers. If you're blessed, you might even have a few mentors who help guide you in a wise, godly way. Yet as much as teachers and mentors are wonderful, they won't always be with you.

Even without teachers, you still can and will be taught. In fact, God will find a way for you to keep learning. He'll make a way to build you up. By using the truth of His Word and life experiences, God will help you know and understand more of His grace. As you're made strong in Him, it will become your turn to pass along His truth to others.

Father, please help me keep learning the message of Your grace. Please continue to build me up in You!

Waiting

Everything that has been made in the world is waiting for the day when God will make His sons known. Everything that has been made in the world is weak. It is not that the world wanted it to be that way. God allowed it to be that way. Yet there is hope.

ROMANS 8:19–20

Waiting isn't an easy thing. Especially if you tend to be impatient, it can feel really, really hard and frustrating to wait for a big event or privilege.

Yet all of creation is waiting for something even bigger: the day when Jesus will return. All of creation will finally be freed from the imperfections and pain that sin brings. Nothing will decay anymore. Nothing will die. Creation will live in freedom, and every part of creation will praise the Lord.

Until that day, creation waits in hope. You can too!

Father, please help me wait patiently for Jesus' return. I can't imagine life without death or decay, but it sounds amazingly wonderful! What freedom!

Peace!

"You will keep the man in perfect peace whose mind is kept on You, because he trusts in You."
Isaiah 26:3

You might set your mind to work hard at school or determine to practice until a skill becomes second nature. In fact, you can set your mind on anything.

If you choose to set your mind on Christ and fully trust Him, worries of this world won't faze you. You'll know that God is in control of all and that you don't have to be concerned about what might happen. He has a plan, and you can walk confidently in it.

When you put your complete trust in Christ, you have an absence of worries and a sense of perfect peace. Your concerns fade as you experience a true peace you can't explain. All of that perfect peace comes as a result of your faithful trust in Christ.

Lord Jesus, I trust in You! I want to set my mind on You to experience peace. Besides, I know You are worthy of my complete trust!

Stuck in the Middle

You, O Lord, are a covering around me, my shining-greatness, and the One Who lifts my head. I was crying to the Lord with my voice. And He answered me from His holy mountain.

PSALM 3:3–4

Everyone goes through difficult times. You might be in a tough spot right now, where it seems like absolutely everything is going wrong.

When you're in the middle of the storms of life, cry out to God! Tell Him every one of your complaints. Admit that you're weak or afraid or frustrated or mad. Tell Him all your fears and feelings.

As you're honest, not only will God listen, but He'll also respond. He'll answer your prayers and protect you, just like a shield. He'll be your shining greatness in the middle of the dark days of life. And He'll lift and hold your head high. Whenever you feel like you're stuck in the middle of problems, call out to God. He will hear and He will help.

Father, thank You for being so kind and faithful to help me when I need You most!

Changes

As you have put your trust in Christ Jesus the Lord to save you from the punishment of sin, now let Him lead you in every step. Have your roots planted deep in Christ. Grow in Him. Get your strength from Him. Let Him make you strong in the faith as you have been taught. Your life should be full of thanks to Him.

COLOSSIANS 2:6–7

When you accepted Christ Jesus as your Lord, a huge change happened: You stepped from death to life. You had been separated from God because of your sins, but now you're forgiven and free.

The changes didn't stop at that moment though. In fact, you'll keep changing and growing the rest of your life. As you learn more and more about Jesus and His truth, you can build your life on Him through obedience. You can establish deep roots in Him so your life won't be shaken. Your faith will grow stronger and stronger the longer you're part of Christ.

Lord, I want to keep learning from You and growing closer to You! Please help me become more and more like You.

No Worries

Do not worry. Learn to pray about everything. Give thanks to God as you ask Him for what you need. The peace of God is much greater than the human mind can understand. This peace will keep your hearts and minds through Christ Jesus.

PHILIPPIANS 4:6–7

Focusing on anxious thoughts comes naturally for some people. They may even brag about their worries by telling everyone, "I'm a worrier!" But you don't have to worry. In fact, the Bible tells you to stop worrying!

So what can replace your worries? Prayer! When you pray, thank God for as many things as possible. Honestly tell Him everything that's on your mind. In return, His peace will come rushing to the scene to guard your heart and mind from worry. You won't be able to understand why or how it works, but when it does work, be sure to thank your heavenly Father!

Father God, thank You for Your peace! I can't understand it, but I'm so thankful for the way it calms me down and guards my heart and mind.

Absolutely Nothing

Who can keep us away from the love of Christ? Can trouble or problems? Can suffering wrong from others or having no food? Can it be because of no clothes or because of danger or war?

Romans 8:35

Sometimes it seems like a lot of things in life could or should separate you from Christ's love.

Hardship could drive a wedge between you and Christ's love, right? No. Nothing can separate you from His love.

Facing troubles or being persecuted for your faith would put a strain on your relationship with Christ, right? No! Nothing can separate you from His love.

How about big troubles in life—like being so poor that you run out of food or clothing? Or what if natural disasters come and wipe everything away? Could those separate you from the love of Christ? No! Nothing can separate you from His love.

No matter what you face in this life, you can conquer any obstacle and still experience the never-ending love of Christ.

Jesus, thank You for loving me! The fact that absolutely nothing can separate me from Your love is a wonderful gift.

My Plans versus God's Purpose

There are many plans in a man's heart,
but it is the Lord's plan that will stand.
PROVERBS 19:21

New Year's resolutions are popular to talk about—if you set a bunch of goals at the beginning of a year, it seems like you can be really successful. But how many resolutions fizzle and fade away a couple of weeks after they're made?

It's really easy to make plans, set goals, and create resolutions, but in the end, they're a lot like wishes and dreams. What really makes a difference? The purpose and plans of the Lord. Those are the plans that'll actually happen and succeed.

But it's not as if your plans or hopes are bad—in fact, it's good to try to improve weak areas of your life. But instead of believing that they absolutely have to come true, hold them with an open hand. Pray for the Lord's guidance and directions, make some goals or plans, then try to go with the flow and see if your plans end up being God's plans too!

Father, please give me direction for my life.

Show It!

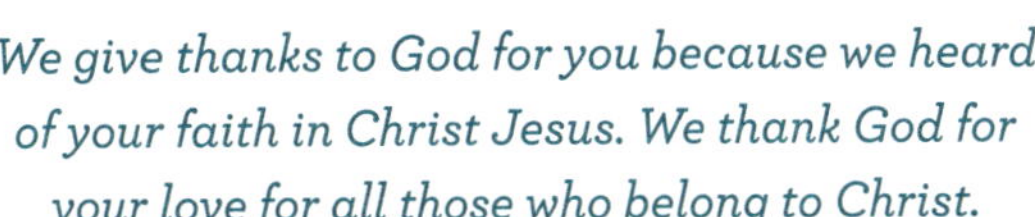

We give thanks to God for you because we heard of your faith in Christ Jesus. We thank God for your love for all those who belong to Christ.

COLOSSIANS 1:4

Have you ever met someone who ended up completely surprising you? Maybe she acted one way or said certain things, and then you were shocked to find out she was someone else. Saying or acting one way and then revealing you believe something completely different isn't an authentic way of living. In fact, it's totally fake.

If you love and trust Christ, it's time to start living like it. Jesus told His followers to love others—not only fellow believers, but also people who don't believe in Him and are far from a Christian life.

As you live a life of love, you'll show your belief and trust in Christ. You'll show you're serious about your relationship with Him. You'll show that your faith is authentic and the real deal.

Lord Jesus, I want to be known for my faith in You! Please help me love others the way You've asked.

Smile!

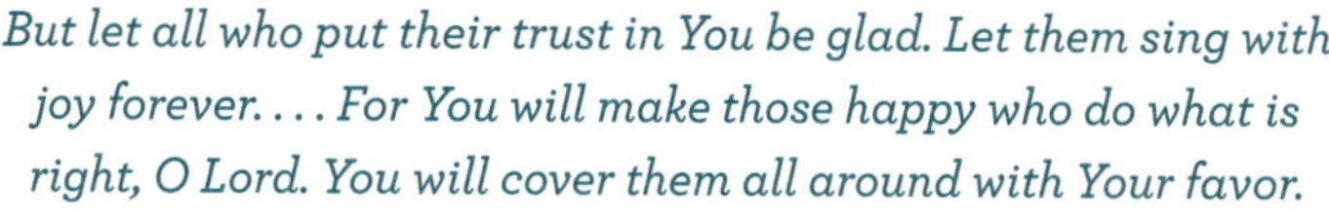

But let all who put their trust in You be glad. Let them sing with joy forever. . . . For You will make those happy who do what is right, O Lord. You will cover them all around with Your favor.

Psalm 5:11–12

When you think about all the Lord has done for you and all you have through Him, you should be really glad!

You can be happy when you remember that God protects you and showers you with His favor! You can be really, truly glad to remember that God is your safe place and that you can run to Him for shelter when it feels like your heart is breaking or you're scared.

Through Christ, you're made right with God. And with that rightness, God begins to bless you. He won't just bless you, but He'll also surround you with His favor. To know you're surrounded with God's favor? That's something to make you smile!

Father, thank You for Your really wonderful gifts! Thanks for surrounding me with Your favor! Thanks for protecting me! I want to be glad in You!

Encouraged

Our Lord Jesus Christ and God our Father loves us. Through His loving-favor He gives us comfort and hope that lasts forever. May He give your hearts comfort and strength to say and do every good thing.

2 THESSALONIANS 2:16–17

Everyone can use encouragement. Even the most confident people in the world still struggle with insecurity—they just might hide their feelings really well. But as uncertain as people might feel, encouragement does a wonderful job at silencing doubts.

Encouragement simply means to inspire with hope and courage. Jesus can strengthen your spirit and encourage your heart, but you have to pay attention to how He does it. The Lord may speak to you through His Word or by what someone else says or does. He might encourage you through your circumstances or through an obvious blessing or answered prayer.

Keep looking for the good that God is working in your life, and feel encouraged!

Lord, thank You for Your love and hope. I want to keep my eyes focused on You and the many ways You're blessing me!

When Disaster Strikes

"The mountains may be taken away and the hills may shake, but My loving-kindness will not be taken from you. And My agreement of peace will not be shaken," says the Lord who has loving-pity on you.

Isaiah 54:10

Nothing can seem to rock your world quite like a catastrophe. Natural disasters seem to bring the world to a screeching halt. Sickness can add a huge pause to your daily life. When tragedy strikes, all that's normal stops for a while.

In the middle of the worst moments, remember that nothing changes the way God loves or cares for you. Nothing switches His never-ending promises. He still is God; no circumstance changes the reality of who He is. No matter what, you can continue to trust and worship Him. You can continue to experience His love and His peace, even in your darkest days. When disaster strikes, God still is watching out for you!

Lord, I know that no one can escape awful days. When I'm faced with difficulties, please help me experience Your love and peace in very real ways.

The Power of Peace

Let the peace of Christ have power over your hearts.
You were chosen as a part of His body. Always be thankful.
COLOSSIANS 3:15

When everyone focuses on differences and picking sides of "right" and "wrong," peace seems impossible. When mean people gang up and bully others with actions or words, peace feels out of reach. When fear spreads and worries multiply, peace feels hopeless.

Peace won't happen in a worldly way, where everyone gets along in total agreement. Yet peace is possible through Christ. As He taught during His life on earth, Jesus promised, "Peace I leave with you. My peace I give to you" (John 14:27).

Without Christ, you'll never experience His peace. But with Jesus ruling in your heart and in your life, His peace that can't fully be understood or explained will guard your heart and mind. Because of His peace, you can live in peace with others.

Lord Jesus, You give me peace. Thank You!
Please always calm my worries and my fears.
May I trust in You and rest in Your peace.

Getting Stronger

The Lord is my strength and my safe cover.
My heart trusts in Him, and I am helped. So my heart
is full of joy. I will thank Him with my song.
PSALM 28:7

If you've ever tried to become physically stronger, you know it doesn't happen instantly. It takes time and a lot of work and practice to build muscles and grow stronger.

Similarly, your spiritual muscles also need time, work, and practice to get stronger. The more you trust the Lord, the stronger you and your faith will become. When you trust Him, He'll help you. He'll protect you like a shield, and He'll strengthen you to stand up against evil schemes and attacks.

Be sure to thank and praise Him for what He's doing in your life. And celebrate! It makes God happy to know He's filling you with joy. As you get stronger, make sure you praise and celebrate even more.

Lord, I'm so glad You are my strength
and my safe cover! I trust You completely.
Thank You for Your help and for filling me with joy.

Part of a Family

Now the God Who helps you not to give up and gives you strength will help you think so you can please each other as Christ Jesus did. Then all of you together can thank the God and Father of our Lord Jesus Christ.

ROMANS 15:5–6

When you belong to Christ, you become part of His family—with countless other people who belong to Christ too. You're not alone. You have brothers and sisters in Christ. And just as in any family, it's important to treat each other with love and respect.

Just like earthly families, sometimes you need to put a lot of effort into getting along with each other. The good news is that God doesn't leave you on your own to figure things out. He gives you strength and ideas. Through Him, you can try to treat your brothers and sisters in Christ like Jesus would treat them!

Father, I'm so glad I'm part of Your family! Please help me honor You in the way I treat my brothers and sisters in Christ.

He Loved Me First

We love Him because He loved us first. If a person says, "I love God," but hates his brother, he is a liar. If a person does not love his brother whom he has seen, how can he love God Whom he has not seen?

1 JOHN 4:19–20

Love is woven throughout the entire Bible. God loved the world so much that He gave His only Son. His Son, Jesus, lived a life of love and taught His followers that love should be their trademark.

Your love for others should come oozing out of you because it's God's love. You don't have to love in your own strength or by your own will. But God can use you to let His love pour out on this broken world. Because He loved you first, you can love others in your life—whether they seem completely lovable or unlovable.

Lord, Your love for me is so amazingly wonderful and generous and never-ending. Thank You! I love You! Please help me show my love for You by loving others too.

The Sting of Rejection

"I let Myself be looked for by those who did not ask for Me. I let Myself be found by those who did not look for Me. I said, 'Here I am, here I am,' to a nation that did not call on My name. All day long I held out My hand to a people who would not obey Me and who worked against Me."

ISAIAH 65:1–2

How do you feel when someone ignores you? Have you felt hurt? Or invisible?

Believe it or not, God knows how you feel. He has felt like it before, and He still feels like it. Whenever people choose to overlook Him, ridicule Him, or refuse to think about Him or give Him credit, God knows the hurt.

Even when He faces rejection, God still opens His arms, ready to welcome people in. Some people (hopefully *you*!) hear Him and come running, ready for His help and open arms. But others keep choosing to ignore Him, rebel against Him, or reject Him. How do you choose to respond to Him?

Lord, You're ready to be found, even when people turn from You. Thank You!

Known

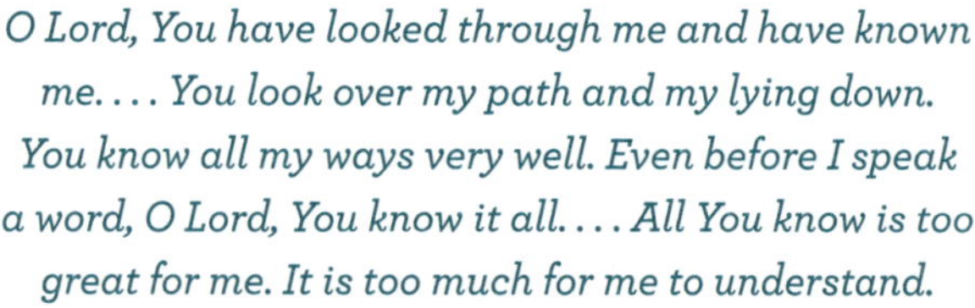

O Lord, You have looked through me and have known me. . . . You look over my path and my lying down. You know all my ways very well. Even before I speak a word, O Lord, You know it all. . . . All You know is too great for me. It is too much for me to understand.

PSALM 139:1, 3–4, 6

Whether or not you believe it, you're a fascinating person. (Really! You are!) If someone else would take the time to get to know the real you with all of your hopes and fears and strengths and even your weaknesses, that would be great. What would be even better? If someone knew you completely and chose to love you.

Here's some amazing news: Someone does know every single detail about you and loves you completely. That special someone is your heavenly Father. Even if you're surprised that He knows absolutely everything about you and still loves you, He does!

Father, it's amazing to realize how well You know me. And the fact that You love me too? Wow! I'm in awe.

Never Turned Away

"All whom My Father has given to Me will come to Me. I will never turn away anyone who comes to Me. . . . He wants everyone who sees the Son to put his trust in Him and have life that lasts forever."

JOHN 6:37, 40

It can be easy to think of God with human traits. If humans are moody and change their minds, wouldn't God? But instead of thinking that God is like humans, remember that humans are created in God's image. They should reflect Him. God doesn't reflect humans.

Once you believe in Christ and trust Him completely, forever life is waiting for you. You don't have to worry about God changing His mind every time you sin. You don't have to worry if your salvation really is legit. God the Father knows all believers—He has chosen them and knows they will come to Christ. When they do come to Him, they'll never be turned away.

Lord, I don't deserve forever life, but I'm so glad You've offered it to me through Jesus! Thanks for choosing me. I pray I'll always stay close to You.

Not Your Own

Do you not know that your body is a house of God where the Holy Spirit lives? God gave you His Holy Spirit. Now you belong to God. You do not belong to yourselves. God bought you with a great price. So honor God with your body. You belong to Him.

1 CORINTHIANS 6:19–20

Think about the best thing you've ever purchased. Whether it's a pet or a favorite keepsake, it belongs to you because you paid for it.

In the same way, Christ bought you at a great price: His very life. Because He paid such a costly price for you, you matter to Him. You don't belong to yourself, but to Him. Since you're His valuable belonging, you should live like it.

Instead of pretending that you can choose to do anything you please, remember the cost Christ paid. Then make choices that will make Him happy. Please Him with your body—from the things you do with your body to the things you do to your body. You have just one life and one body—use them to show that you belong to the Lord!

Lord, help me honor You with my body!

Selfless

Do not always be thinking about your own plans only.
Be happy to know what other people are doing.
PHILIPPIANS 2:4

It can be really easy to stay self-centered and focus on what you like or what makes you happy. Do you feel comfortable? What do you feel like doing right now? Does this make you feel good?

But what about other people? There are many big issues that come with being self-centered; maybe the major one is that being self-centered is all about being selfish. When your focus is all about you and what brings you happiness and comfort, you tune out everyone else.

Christ calls us to be like Himself: loving, humble, and selfless. Instead of being focused on what you're interested in, take a genuine interest in others too. When you do, you'll find that your heart will grow.

Lord Jesus, please help me to be more like You! I want to take my eyes off myself. Please help me look to You—and others!

No One Else

From long ago no ear has heard and no eye has seen any God besides You, Who works for those who wait for Him. You meet him who finds joy in doing what is right and good, who remembers You in Your ways. See, You were angry because we sinned. We have been sinning for a long time, and will we be saved?

Isaiah 64:4–5

Have you ever considered that there's not a single person or thing that is like God? No one else works for those who wait for Him like God does. No one else welcomes those who follow godly ways. No one else offers to forgive those who fall short of perfection and run into sin.

But God does. God made a way for you to be forgiven and saved. That way is through Jesus, who came to earth and didn't hide the fact that He is the Way, the Truth, and the Life (John 14:6). No one comes to the Father but through Him.

Lord Jesus, I worship You! You are the Way, the Truth, and the Life, and I believe in You and trust You!

Hope for the Weary

"I will help the tired ones and give strength to everyone who is weak."

JEREMIAH 31:25

Are you feeling stressed out or worn out? You might have troubles at school or concerns about your family or drama with friends.

The antidote to being worn out by troubles is spending time with your heavenly Father. Tell Him what's zapping your energy, strength, and thoughts. Be honest about your worries. Then get into His Word and see what He has to say. Spend time reading and pondering the Bible. Read just one verse or one paragraph or one chapter of the Bible and ask yourself what it says. What do you observe? What does it mean? How can you apply that one bit of scripture to your life right now?

As you spend time with the Lord, you'll discover that He's the one who will satisfy and replenish your weary soul.

Father, I'm tired. I'm worn out. I can't keep going on my own. I pray that You'll give me strength!

One

"I do not pray for these followers only. I pray for those who will put their trust in Me through the teaching they have heard. May they all be as one, Father, as You are in Me and I am in You. May they belong to Us. Then the world will believe that You sent Me."

JOHN 17:20–21

Did you know that before Jesus faced the cross, He prayed specifically for you? His friend and disciple John detailed some of Jesus' final prayers, and Jesus prayed for *you*.

Wonder what He prayed about? He prayed that you'd be one with other believers. That means it's important for you to live in unity with other Christ followers. The world is full of people with different opinions, but those who follow Christ have one major thing in common: their Lord! Because of that, living in unity is so important.

Today you can become the answer to Jesus' prayer: Stay united with other believers!

Lord Jesus, it's amazing You prayed for me in Your last hours on earth. Please help me to be unified with my Christian brothers and sisters.

Scripture Index

OLD TESTAMENT

NEW TESTAMENT

Acts

Romans

1 Corinthians

2 Corinthians

Galatians

Ephesians

All Praise

Even before the world was made, God chose us for Himself because of His love. He planned that we should be holy and without blame as He sees us. God already planned to have us as His own children. This was done by Jesus Christ. In His plan God wanted this done.

EPHESIANS 1:4–5

Do you know what God has done for you through Christ? He loved you even before He made the world. He chose you to be in Christ—that meant He'd see you as being holy and without blame. He decided to adopt you, an outsider, into His own family. He brought you to Himself through Jesus Christ.

Doing all of those things for you and treating you that way brought Him great pleasure. That should bring you great pleasure too! And it should fill your heart, your mind, and your mouth with praise. Praise God, the Father of your Lord Jesus Christ!

Father, I praise You! Thank You for choosing me and planning so many outrageously wonderful things for me. I worship You!